T0156874

# REFORMATION TO
# RESTORATION

The Restoration Ideal in Europe from the
16th to the 19th Century and the Rise of
New Testament Churches in Britain and
America with a Special Focus on Scotland

John Renwick

iUniverse, Inc.
New York   Bloomington

Reformation to Restoration
The Restoration Ideal in Europe from the 16th to the
19th Century and the Rise of New Testament Churches
in Britain and America with a Special Focus on Scotland

*iUniverse books may be ordered through booksellers or by contacting:*

*iUniverse
1663 Liberty Drive
Bloomington, IN 47403
www.iuniverse.com
1-800-Authors (1-800-288-4677)*

*Because of the dynamic nature of the Internet, any Web addresses or links
contained in this book may have changed since publication and may no longer be
valid. The views expressed in this work are solely those of the author and do not
necessarily reflect the views of the publisher, and the publisher hereby disclaims
any responsibility for them.*

*ISBN: 978-1-4502-2411-6 (pbk)
ISBN: 978-1-4502-2412-3 (ebook)*

*Printed in the United States of America*

*iUniverse rev. date: 4/27/10*

To My Beloved Irene

# PREFACE

The attitude of men and women toward the Bible is one of the most interesting and important aspects of church history. To take the Bible as our sole guide and authority in all religious matters is a noble objective. To do so in practice is more difficult, yet it can be done. This work is an attempt to trace the struggle for the truth of God's Word in a European context and particularly in Great Britain from the sixteenth century to the present day. Truth is important. I shall always be grateful to those who taught me the truth of the Gospel, who encouraged me in preaching and interested me in church history. Without their help and encouragement, I could not have written this work and to them I say 'thank you.' It is also appropriate that I should express my appreciation to my wife and my family for their patience and encouragement.

The work is set forth with a spirit of deep concern for the divisions within Christendom. It is my fervent plea that each reader will re-examine their religious viewpoint and submit it to the test of God's Word. Then, may God grant us the courage to make change appropriately and accordingly. I believe it is only in this way, by supreme respect for the

Scriptures and their authority, that we can please God and achieve Christian unity.

Before beginning our story, the writer owes the reader a word on how this material is organised and why. The book has three parts. Part one gives some information on how Christianity came to the British Isles. This is given because it is not only interesting but also because it is not generally known. However, it is only dealt with here in the briefest outline, as it is not our primary concern. It would bear much more research by future church historians. Part two gives some European backgrounds to the Reformation. The Protestant Reformation has been dealt with in detail by many accomplished church historians and their work is widely available to readers. We will not therefore dwell on the mainstream Reformation. Where we do want to focus is the Radical Reformation. It has not been widely covered but it has a direct bearing on one of the key aspects of our study, the idea of 'restoration.' Part three goes on to focus on this idea of restoration and that specifically in Britain and in Scotland. From there, restoration principles have had a profound effect on the idea of restoring New Testament Christianity particularly in the U.S.A. and from there on to every continent where man dwells.

Today, people who claim the Restoration ideal are to be found not only in Europe and North America but also in Australia, in Africa, in South America and in Asia. Congregations can be found in well over a hundred countries and the number of members runs to millions. This study is part of their heritage.

John Renwick
Stirling, Scotland
2004

# CONTENTS

# PART ONE

–

# EUROPE: BACKGROUNDS OF REFORMATION

# CHAPTER 1

# CHURCH HISTORY: ANCIENT AND MEDIEVAL

## The Church of the Britons

'When did Christianity arrive in the British Isles?' Traditionally church historians look to Celtic missionaries of the fifth and sixth centuries. However, Nennius and Geoffrey of Monmouth provide a tantalizing glimpse of a much earlier scenario. Nennius and Geoffrey were British monks and historians, Nennius in the ninth century and Geoffrey in the eleventh century. They left a fascinating record. The story goes like this: In the middle of the first century A.D., a succession of kings, Llyr, Bran, Caradog (also known as Caractacus or Caratacus), Cyllin, Coel and Lleirwig ruled the Britons in Cambria (Wales). They recorded some of their histories as poetry, each verse being of three lines, hence the name 'triads.' Two of these poems tell us that "Bran was seven years a hostage in Rome for his son Caradog." Caradog ruled the Britons for Rome, his father being the guarantee of co-operation and good behaviour according to standard Roman practice. The seven years that Bran was in Rome were from 51 to 58. From the Epistle to the Romans, written by the Apostle Paul in 58, it is evident that Christianity had a strong hold in the capital of the empire, even in Caesar's household where Bran was a hostage. When Bran was released, in the year 58, he returned to Britain and it was he who "brought the faith of Christ to the Cambrians" (the Welsh Britons). Flinders Petrie, the eminent archaeologist, attested to this record in a paper on 'Neglected British History' delivered to the British Academy in 1917.

In his book 'After the Flood' Bill Cooper concurs with Flinders Petrie: *"It is unequivocally stated in the early records that the man who first brought the Christian faith to these shores was none other than Bran, the father of Caratacus (Caradog) who, with his family, was taken to Rome in chains and paraded before the Senate by the Emperor Claudius with the view to their immediate and summary execution. Caratacus (or, more usually, Caractacus), however, gave his famous speech of defiance that earned him instead the Senate's applause, a state pension and apartments in the Imperial Palace. And here conventional history loses sight of him. But the triads add to our knowledge. They tell us that, in perfect accord with previous Roman practice, Caratacus was allowed home to rule as a puppet king, but his family was kept behind as surety for his good behaviour. Whilst detained for seven years in Caesar's household, his father Bran was converted to Christ and when allowed to return to Britain in AD 58, the very year of Paul's epistle to the Romans, he brought the Christian faith with him. It is difficult to imagine a more straightforward, uncomplicated and entirely feasible account, and we can only wonder why it has been ignored all these years."* We therefore conclude that Christianity first came to the ancient Britons of Wales in the first century through the family of Caradog or Caractacus, the king.

Another poem recorded that the great-grandson of Caradog, Lleirwig, "first gave lands and privilege of the country to those who first dedicated themselves to the faith of Christ" (this being about 130-160). Flinders Petrie commented, "That Christianity was firmly established in even the remotest parts of Britain at the close of the second century is shown by Tertullian stating that 'The Britons in parts inaccessible to the Romans, Christ has truly subdued.'" Origen, writing after Tertullian, also testified to this.

Later, sometime between 170 and 180, the British king Lles or Lucius in the Latin, sent to Eleutherius, bishop of Rome, requesting missioners or teachers. Bede, Tysilio and the Anglo-Saxon Chronicles all mention this as well as the Liber Pontificalis, a series of short Papal biographies. The entry in the Anglo-Saxon Chronicles for the year 167 records: *Eleutherius received the bishopric in Rome and held it worthily for fifteen years. To him Lucius, King of the Britons, sent men with letters, asking that he be baptized and he soon sent back to him; after this they remained in the true faith until Diocletian's time.*

British bishops attended the Council of Arles in France in 314, convened by the emperor Constantine to resolve the Donatist controversy. This followed the new emperor's Edict of Milan in 313 and preceded the Council of Nicea by a decade. The fact that the church of the ancient Britons sent bishops to the council shows that early in the fourth century the church was both organised and mature. Not only that but the church in continental Europe recognised its organisation, maturity and authority.

The presence of a Roman chapel at Canterbury dedicated to the Frankish missionary, Martin (d.397), is also indicative of early Christianity. Again Bede, the eighth century ecclesiastical historian, records that: *After Augustine had, as we said before, received his episcopate see in the royal city, he with the help of the king restored a church in it, which, as he was informed, had been built in ancient times by the hands of the Roman believers.* When Augustine arrived in Britain in 597, Ethelbert was king of Kent. Ethelbert married a Frankish princess, Bertha. She held the Christian faith and with the aid of her bishop, Liudhard, she was allowed to practice Christianity. She used this chapel, the foundation of which goes back to Roman times. This would certainly be before the year 400.

Around the year 400, Pelagius was in Rome. He was a British monk and scholar, opposed by Augustine of Hippo in the famous Pelagian controversy. Evidently the church of the ancient Britons was producing scholars of world renown even before the missions of Patrick, Ninian and Columba. We have noted evidence for Christianity in Britain in the first, second and fourth centuries based on the testimony of history. Other historians cite Christian art in Roman villas such as Lullingstone in Kent, as evidence for Christianity in Britain in the third century. The fifth and sixth centuries provide us with more evidence.

The ancestors of the ancient Britons arrived in the Britain late in the second millennium B.C. Christianity arrived on their shores in the middle of the first century A.D. The faith of Christ was part of Great Britain along with the Roman legions of that time. Other historical records testify of Christianity in Scotland in the fifth century. It was to follow the pattern of Christianity found among the ancient Britons. We know this as Celtic Christianity as opposed to Roman Christianity. The Celts migrated to Britain and Ireland from central Europe via the Iberian Peninsula and Brittany after 500 B.C. They settled throughout Ireland and on the western fringes of Great Britain. By the end of the fourth century, the ancient Britons had followed

Christianity for hundreds of years. The new mission was to take Christianity to these Celtic peoples. Patrick, Ninian and Columba took up this work in Ireland and Scotland. In the north of Britain, three fascinating ancient centres of Christianity remain today. The first is Whithorn, the second, Iona and the third, Lindisfarne.

Whithorn is where Ninian (c.360-432) established his Casa Candida, 'the white house,' also known as 'the shining place.' He was a contemporary of Patrick of Ireland and Teilo and Illfyd of Wales and shared in the mission of taking Christianity to the northern Britons and Celts in the fifth and sixth centuries. Bede records that Ninian was educated in Rome and the monastery of Martin at Tours in France. He came to Whithorn in the southwest of Scotland about 397. He came as a bishop so it is likely that a Christian community already existed. From there he and others evangelised in southwest Scotland, central Scotland (what today constitutes the central lowlands between Edinburgh and Glasgow) and eastern Scotland.

Iona was where Columba (521-597) began his mission outreach. He came from Patrick's Ireland. Patrick (c.389-461) was probably born in Roman Britain. His family were part of the church of the Britons. After capture, enslavement and escape from Ireland he returned there in 432 and spent the rest of his life in the ministry of the Gospel. He founded the Celtic church in Ireland. This was the background of Columba. In 565, he left Ireland and set up a monastic community on the island of Iona, off the Isle of Mull on the west coast of Scotland. From there Columba and others evangelised in the west and the north of Scotland. He brought the Celtic church to the British tribes of the north, the kingdoms of the people the Romans had called the Picts as well as the newer arrivals in western

Scotland, the Celts. Kentigern or Mungo continued the work of Columba from his base in Glasgow.

Lindisfarne was an offshoot of Iona. In 633, Oswald, ruler of the Northumbrian kingdom of the Britons, sent to Iona for teachers for his people. They sent Aidan and in 635, he set up a monastic community on Lindisfarne, a small island off the northeast coast of England. From there he and others evangelised in southeast Scotland and northeast England. From Lindisfarne the monasteries of the Borders were founded, Melrose, Dryburgh and Jedburgh.

Around the year 450, a third group arrived in the British Isles to join the Britons and the Celts. These were the Angles and the Saxons who migrated to eastern England from northern Germany. By Aidan's time, the immigration of these Angles and Saxons was considerable and he evangelised among them as well as among the Britons. Later Cuthbert continued the work of Aidan.

In the early centuries, Celtic Christianity permeated every part of the British Isles. We use the term 'Celtic Christianity' to describe the church of the Britons and the Celts in Britain and in Ireland. The arrival of the pagan Angles and Saxons in the east pushed the Britons and the Celts back towards the west. Then Augustine arrived, not Augustine of Hippo the famous scholar, but Augustine the missionary and representative of Gregory the Great. Gregory, the leader of the Roman Catholic Church, sent a mission team to the Anglo-Saxons of Great Britain. Augustine and forty monks arrived in Kent in 597. He became the first Archbishop of Canterbury. (Canterbury remains the ecclesiastical seat of the Archbishop of Canterbury today, the leader of the Church of England.) He secured control of religion for the Papacy and brought the British Isles into the Roman

Catholic fold. He did this by every means he could including persuasion, negotiation and coercion. Bede tells us that the native church resisted Roman rule. Traditional church history does not generally record the slaughter of hundreds of monks at Bangor, north Wales as Saxons fought Britons. It is recorded in Bede and in the Anglo-Saxon Chronicles. The slaughter occurred in the year 604. The finest scholars of the church of the Welsh Britons died. With their death, the records of the ancient Britons and their church almost perished. Augustine chose the winning side and in the end he prevailed. Though Augustine died about this time, claims of apostolic succession and the supremacy of Rome were accepted and the issue was sealed at the Synod of Whitby, in northeast England, in 664. From that time, the church in the British Isles would be firmly Roman Catholic. The old Celtic church survived in remote parts of Britain into the tenth century and finally died out by the time of the Norman Conquest in 1066.

Roman missionaries and monks continued to maintain the British church under the control of the Papacy. Unfortunately, the form of the Roman church was not the form of the church we find in the New Testament. That Christianity came at all to a small country on the edge of the world is remarkable. That it came in a corrupt state is not so. In the first century, the Scriptures warned that people would "turn away from the truth" and that they would "depart from the faith." This happened as surely as the Word of God stands. From approximately 600 to 1500 the British Isles were Roman Catholic. This period encompasses what is sometimes referred to as 'the Dark Ages.' This era is not our concern here. There has been a constant struggle to maintain the purity of Christianity from the earliest times. In Europe, it came to a head in the sixteenth century. The struggle for truth and the emergence of the faith and practice of the church of the New Testament can be traced from these times. After its arrival in Scotland, the Roman system of Christianity held sway for almost a thousand years. Clearly, a system so entrenched and so dominant would be difficult to overthrow. However, it was overthrown! The movement which accomplished the task shook the whole continent of Europe. We know it as 'the Reformation.' It transformed Scotland in the first half of the sixteenth century. Two hundred years before that, in 1314, Scotland's political freedom had been secured by Robert the Bruce and a valiant generation of Scots on the field of Bannockburn near Stirling. This is important in that it gave Scotland the opportunity to take its own path towards religious freedom. The struggle for religious freedom in these islands began with the Reformation but continues in a very vital sense to this day.

### Reformation Roots
### Movements Preceding the Reformation

Most church historians reckon there was something seriously wrong with the Roman Catholic Church about the time of Martin Luther. He saw the corruption in Rome first hand on a visit in 1510 but Luther reckoned the malaise of the Medieval Roman Church went back to the eighth century. One thing is certain, the Reformation did not just appear from nowhere in the early 16th century. The Reformation had roots in events going back centuries.

In 1347, the first wave of the Black Death swept through Europe. The plague killed one third of the population of Western Europe. In 1354, the Turks crossed the Bosphorus and threatened Europe for a hundred years. Constantinople or Byzantium (present-day Istanbul) fell to the Turks in

1453, thus ending a long and illustrious role as the capital of the eastern Roman Empire and the seat of the Eastern (Orthodox) Church. For Christendom this was an earth-shaking event ending over a thousand years of learning and civilisation based on the Bible. Knowledge and learning were preserved albeit Muslim knowledge and learning as Constantinople became the capital of the Muslim Ottoman Empire, separate from and opposed to Christian Europe. Far from being in the ascendancy, 14th century Europe was fighting for survival, but then came the Renaissance.

'Renaissance' is a term coined by 19th century historians to describe changes that occurred in 14th and 15th century Europe. It was based on a revival of the values of classical Greek and Roman civilisation. It originated in Italy but soon spread throughout Western Europe. The foot soldiers of Renaissance were the humanists. Originally, the term referred to teachers of Latin but it came to mean all those who studied and adopted classical ideas from Greek and Roman culture. The first humanist scholar was Lovato Lovati of Padua (1241-1309). The first famous humanist was Francesco Petrarcha or Petrarch (1304-74). He was a Bible believer. Because of his outlook and his pursuit and appreciation of the aesthetic, he is widely regarded as 'the first modern man.' Humanists collected and preserved copies of many ancient documents by classical writers including copies of the work of the inspired writers of the Old and New Testament. They revived the classical languages, Greek and Latin. Lorenzo Valla of Rome (1405-57) became 'the Father of Biblical Criticism,' a system of analysis whereby the text and the meaning of the Bible could be determined by scrutinising manuscript evidence. He proved the Roman Catholic document, the Donation of Constantine, was a forgery. By 'the Donation' the Papacy claimed the land of the Vatican state, maintaining that it had been given to them by the Roman Emperor Constantine. Valla foreshadowed Erasmus, the greatest of the humanist scholars. Other famous humanists included Giovanni Boccaccio (1313-75), Coluccio Salutari of Florence (1331-1406), Leonardo Bruni (1374-1444), Poggio Bracciolini (1380-1459) of Florence and Rome, Cardinal Bessarion (1395-1472), Emanuel Chrysolas (1350-1415, a Byzantine scholar from Constantinople) and Angelo Poliziano (1454-94). In 1396, Florence created a professorship of Greek and Chrysolas became the first professor. This would be a very important time in terms of Classical and Biblical studies for until then, very few could read Greek. These and others would lay the foundations for the understanding, translation and study of the Bible in Europe as the Renaissance spread to France, Germany, Holland, Spain and England. In France, the leading humanists were Jacques Lefevre d'Etaples (1450-1536) and Guillaume Bude (1468-1540). In Germany, Johann Reuchlin (1455-1522) established the study of Hebrew in Western Europe. Holland produced the famous Desiderius Erasmus (1467-1536) who published his Greek New Testament in 1516. In Spain, various scholars including Cardinal Ximenez (1436-1517) and Elio Antonio (1440-1522) produced the Polyglot Bible. In England John Colet (1467-1519) and Sir Thomas More (1478-1535) led the way into the new learning. It was to be vital to the huge religious revival of the 16th century that we know as the Reformation. The Scriptures were accessible. They could be checked, translated and studied. People no longer had to rely on and accept the traditions and the teachings of the Roman Catholic Church. They could go back to the Bible and base their faith on the Word of God. In the meantime, changes were occurring not only in the academic realm of learning but also in the religious realm of preaching.

Before the Reformation, Meister Eckhart (1260-1327) a German preacher attracted huge crowds by his powerful sermons. He stirred up the common people and they began to take an interest in religion. His pupil Johann Tauler (1300-61) followed in that tradition. People flocked to hear his preaching. With the publication of Devotio Moderna, 'The modern way of serving God,' spiritual revival began in the Roman Catholic Church in northern Europe. In Holland, Geert Groote (1340-84) paved the way for the establishment of 'the Brethren of the Common Life' and it was set up by his disciple, Florentius Radewyn (1350-1400). It was an order devoted to education and the spiritual life. Thomas Haemarken (1380-1471) was a member of the order. We know him better as Thomas A Kempis. His book, 'The Imitation of Christ,' is a classic and remains a best seller today. The Devotia Moderna and the Brethren of the Common Life made hearts and minds ready to receive the teachings of the Reformers. John Wesel (1400-81), another powerful German preacher, spoke out against the corruption of the Roman Catholic Church. He declared the Bible alone to be the sole authority in religion. In Holland, Wessel Gansfort (1419-89) preached on the same themes Luther would take up. He was educated by the Brethren of the Common Life as was the most famous scholar of all, Desiderius Erasmus of Rotterdam (1467-1536). He was a prodigious writer but his epoch-changing work was the publication of the Greek New Testament. It was printed in Basle, Switzerland in 1516, a year before Luther nailed his famous 95 theses to the door of the church building in Wittenberg. The study of the Bible in its original languages and its translation into the languages of the people precipitated the Reformation.

In the 15th century, two dozen new universities were founded at places as far apart as Alcala, Bordeaux, Tubingen, Wittenberg, St Andrews and Uppsala. Foundations were laid for the great libraries, the Vatican in Rome, the Laurentian in Florence and the Bodleian in Oxford. Then came the invention of the millennium, printing. Printing had been invented in Asia in the 5th century AD. The first book was printed in China in 868. However, movable type had to wait for Johann Gutenberg (1400-68). In Mainz, Germany, he printed the first book, the Bible, using his new method. The year was 1456. Printing presses were then established at Paris in 1470, Rome and Krakow in 1474 and London in 1476. Printing was a vital part of the Reformation. Through the printed word, the writings of Luther and Melancthon reached a wide readership within weeks.

In the meantime, the medieval Roman Catholic Church, particularly its high officials, had sunk to a new low of corruption and immorality. The Medici Pope, Leo X ascended the Papal throne in 1513 and said, "Now that we have attained the Papacy, let us enjoy it." The Fifth Lateran Council of 1512 upheld the status quo even as the floodgates of reformation were bursting wide open in northern Europe.

Martin Luther was born in 1483. He was five years old when Diaz sailed round the Cape of Good Hope. He was 9 years old when Christopher Columbus discovered America. He was 15 years old when Vasco Da Gamma went to India. Within his lifetime, the world witnessed the expeditions of Cabot, Cortez, Magellan and Pizzaro. Spain, France, Holland and England were in the forefront of exploration and colonisation

This was the world that Luther entered and also Zwingli, Calvin and Knox. In those names, we see the foundations of the great Protestant reform movements and the major Protestant denominations. However, remember, they did not just step onto the stage of history and begin their work from nothing. The individuals and movements we have noted, though lesser known and overshadowed by them, went ahead of them. The Protestant reformers followed in reforming footsteps.

# CHAPTER 2

# REFORMATION: MAINSTREAM & RADICAL

## THE REFORMATION

We know the religious tidal wave that burst upon Europe in the 16th century as the Reformation. Every church historian mentions it and many document it very well. However, a note of the central characters, the main ideas and the geographical distribution of the Reformation will be helpful. This outline will cover the mainstream Reformation which conventional church history has treated very fully. However, originating in the mainstream Reformation and running parallel to it is the Radical Reformation. Conventional church histories neglect it but, in the quest for truth, it demands our attention. The mainstream Reformation reformed the corrupt medieval Roman church and brought in the great monolithic state religions of northern European Protestant countries. The Radical Reformation advanced the idea of returning to the Bible and laid the foundations for the Restoration Movement. We begin with a brief sketch of the main characters in the Reformation.

## John Wycliffe (1329-1384)

Church historians know Wycliffe as "The Morning Star of the Reformation." He was a philosopher at Oxford who earned the displeasure of the Roman Catholic Church by speaking out against corrupt clergy. He opposed transubstantiation and the mediation of priests. He would not have survived but friends protected him when the Pope condemned him. Opposition forced him out of Oxford in 1382 and he went to Lutterworth where he died in 1384. He wrote many books and began to translate the Bible into English. His followers were called Lollards, meaning mumblers. They organised themselves into congregations, supported ministers and preached the Bible. They opened the way for the Reformation in England and survived into the early 1600's.

## Martin Luther (1483-1546)

Luther was born in Eisleben, Germany. He studied law at Erfurt and became an Augustinian monk in 1505. Ordained in 1507, he continued his studies in theology and was appointed teacher of Moral Theology at Wittenberg. He visited Rome in 1510-11. In 1512, he qualified as a Doctor of Theology and he was appointed Professor of Biblical Studies at Wittenberg. Because of his own spiritual search, he rejected the doctrine of justification by works and formulated the doctrine of justification by faith. Luther rejected the ideas that the church controls salvation and hands down penance to atone for sin as erroneous and corrupt. He attacked the sale of indulgences. The idea that financial contributions could secure pardon for sin or ameliorate purgatory was repugnant to him. People even bought these in advance as a means of laying up grace. The Papacy needed money to build St Peter's basilica and the sale of Indulgences brought in a great deal of money. In Germany, a priest named Tetzel was a peddler of Indulgences and Luther challenged him. On 31 October 1517, he nailed his famous 95 Theses to the door of the church building in Wittenberg. These were 95 points on which Luther disagreed with the Roman Catholic Church. For example, one said, *'There is no divine authority for preaching that the soul flies out of purgatory as soon as the money clinks in the collecting box.'* He put these up for debate. Luther did not intend to break with his church. When opposition forced him to flee, he went to Augsburg and there debated with Cardinal Cajetan and Bishop Eck. He denied the supremacy of the Pope and the authority of church councils. He was excommunicated in 1521 but refused to recant before the Diet of Worms that same year. Frederick, the Elector of Saxony, incarcerated him in Wartburg castle for his own safety. There he translated the Bible into German. As the Reformation took hold, he returned to Wittenberg. He did away with the mass and stressed communion (consubstantiation), congregational singing and preaching. In 1530, he approved the Augsburg confession of faith drawn up by the man who would become his successor, Philip Melancthon. It was at the Diet of Worms that he said, *'I stand convicted by Scripture ... on this I take my stand. I can do no other. God help me.'* The Holy Roman Emperor, Charles V opposed Luther but many German Princes supported him. At the Diet of Speyer in 1529, the Emperor tried to force Luther to back down but the princes stood up in protest and the name 'Protestant' was born (1500 years after the name Christian).

## Philip Melancthon (1497-1560)

Melancthon met Luther in 1518 and became his disciple and successor. A Professor of Greek at Tubingen and then

Wittenberg, he was a popular preacher and a brilliant theologian. At the Marburg Conference in 1529 he opposed Zwingli over the Swiss reformer's view that communion was a simple memorial. Zwingli rejected the Roman Catholic Church's idea of transubstantiation and Luther's idea of consubstantiation.

## Martin Bucer (1491-1551)

Bucer was a Dominican friar who left the order in 1522 to spearhead the Reformation in Strasburg. He was the great statesman of the movement and a renowned Biblical scholar. He tried to reconcile the views of Luther and Zwingli on the Lord's Supper. He took part in three unsuccessful conferences with the Roman Catholics aimed at reconciliation. In 1549, he had to escape from Strasburg and he fled to Cambridge. There he became a very influential theologian and a forerunner of Puritanism.

## Huldreich Zwingli (1484-1531)

Zwingli was Swiss and educated at Basle, Berne and Vienna in Greek and Church History. He became an army chaplain. He met Erasmus in 1515. In 1518, he became the preacher at the Gross Munster, the great cathedral in Zurich. Working with the city council, he introduced Reformation ideas. In 1522, he married secretly and later had four children. Four other cantons joined the Reformation. Five cantons opposed the reforms. The two sides went to war and Zwingli was killed at the battle of Kappel in 1531. He rejected Catholicism, Lutheranism (because of their different views on communion) and Anabaptism. His major achievement was the establishment of the Reformed Church which, in various forms, would spread to Geneva, Holland and Scotland.

## John Calvin (1509-1564)

Calvin was born in Noyen in Picardy, France. He studied humanities in Paris. Introduced to teachings of Luther and converted in 1533, he broke with Catholicism and settled in Basle, Switzerland. He published his famous treatise, the Institutes of the Christian Religion in 1536. William Farel persuaded him to come to Geneva in 1541 but he was expelled and he went to Strasburg to meet with Bucer before returning to Geneva later that year. There, with the city council, he established a theocratic state. He was a powerful scholar and writer. He tried to build his theology on the foundation of the absolute supremacy and authority of Scripture.

## Theodore Beza (1519-1556)

Beza was a lawyer and disciple of Calvin. He would become Calvin's successor. He became a Greek professor at Lausanne and then Geneva. He worked closely with the French Protestants, the Huguenots.

## Thomas Cranmer (1489-1556)

Cranmer was educated at Cambridge and he became Archbishop of Canterbury in 1532. Henry VIII established the Church of England in 1534. Although the Pope had conferred on him the title 'Defender of the Faith' for writing against Luther, Henry broke with Rome over the issue of divorce. Cranmer, as the senior church official in England, became the architect of the new Church of England. Lutheran in his theology, he was ably supported in that task by the scholar Nicholas Ridley and the preacher Hugh Latimer. Later, all three were burned at the stake under the sovereignty of Henry's reactionary Roman

Catholic daughter, Mary.  When Mary died, Protestantism was re-established by the next monarch, Henry's younger daughter, Elizabeth.

## John Knox (1505-1572)

Knox was born in Haddington, Scotland.  His quarrels with Mary Queen of Scots are legendary.  Lutheran ideas were brought to Scotland by Patrick Hamilton who was burned at the stake by Archbishop Beaton in St Andrews in 1528.  George Wishart and Knox continued Hamilton's work.  In 1547, Knox was taken prisoner by the French and served as a galley slave.  Freed by the English in 1559, he returned to Scotland to launch the Reformation.

This accounts for the countries and states of Germany, Zurich, Geneva, England and Scotland.  They can be summarized under the headings of the reformers.  In other countries, there were no comparable men but the Reformation still took effect.  A brief description is given here country by country.

## Sweden

The king himself, Gustavus Vasa, led the Reformation.  He was aided by two churchmen, the brothers Olav and Lars Petri, who had been students of Luther in Wittenberg.  In 1527, Lutheranism was established as the state church.

## Denmark

Two Danes, Hans Tausen and Jorgen Sadolin, led the Reformation.  They had also studied under Luther at Wittenberg.  The cause was supported by the monarchs Frederick I and Christian III.  By 1536, Lutheranism was established as the state church. From Denmark, Lutheranism spread to Norway and Iceland.

## Central Europe

Today the Czech Republic, Slovakia, Hungary, Austria & Poland.

In the 16th century, Moravia, Bohemia, Prussia, Silesia & Transylvania.

Reform in this part of Europe was prefigured by the work of John Huss (1374-1415). A disciple of Wycliffe, Huss believed and preached the supremacy of Scripture and was very critical of the Roman Church. He attended the Council of Constance in 1415 where he was arrested, condemned and burned as a heretic. After the Reformation, all these areas went over to Lutheran and Calvinist theology. The lands of Moravia and Bohemia were devastated during the 30 Year's War. Austria and Hungary reverted to Catholicism after the Counter-Reformation. So did Poland except for the Polish Brethren under the teaching of Fausto Socinius (1539-1604). Socinianism however denied the doctrine of the Trinity.

## The Netherlands

In Reformation times, Spain ruled the Netherlands. Charles V and Philip II opposed reform. Nevertheless, the ideas of Luther, Zwingli and Calvin took hold. Spanish authorities attacked the newly established Dutch Reformed Church. The Spanish ruler, the Duke of Alva, is reputed to have killed 100,000 Protestants between 1567 and 1573. By 1575, the people of Holland freed themselves from Spanish rule and the Reformation was established by the Synod of

Dort, the same year in which the University of Leiden was founded. There a professor, Jacob Arminius broke with the teaching of Calvin on predestination. He maintained that man had a free will and the doctrine became known as Arminianism.

### France

Reformed ideas were not so popular with the court, the church or the people. Some did go over to the Reformation but they had a real battle. France also had a powerful Roman Catholic neighbour in Spain and supported by the Spanish monarchs, France remained largely Roman Catholic. Cardinal Richelieu was particularly severe on the Protestants who were known as Huguenots. Many had to flee the country.

### Ireland

Ireland had the Reformation imposed upon it by English monarchs. Consequently, the people saw Reformed ideas as the innovation of an oppressor and they never really took hold. However, in the 17th century Protestant Scots were introduced into Ulster by James I. From that time, the political and civil struggles that went with this religious divide have gone on.

There now follows the briefest sketch of what the Protestant Reformation meant for Europe. The reader is referred to any good church history for a fuller discussion of the Reformation.

## What did Protestants stand for?
## They rejected:

The authority of the Pope, the merit of good works, indulgencies, mediation of the Virgin Mary and the saints, all sacraments not instituted by Christ, transubstantiation, the mass as a sacrifice, purgatory, prayers for the dead, private confession of sin to a priest, celibacy of the clergy, use of Latin in services, holy water, shrines, chants, relics, images both icons and statues, rosaries and candles.

## They maintained:

Sola Scriptura - the absolute supremacy and authority of Scripture.  Sola gratia – only by grace.  Salvation is by grace through faith.  Sola fidelis - only by faith.  Justification is by faith not by works.  The priesthood of all believers. They upheld the central role of the Gospel and preaching in man's salvation.

## The five points of Calvinism:

Total hereditary depravity - Unconditional election - Limited atonement - Irresistible grace - Perseverance of the saints.

## The three main traditions of the Protestant Reformation:

Lutheran – (Luther) - Germany and Scandinavia (Sweden, Denmark, Norway)

Reformed or Presbyterian – (Zwingli and Calvin) - Switzerland, Holland and Scotland

Episcopalian or Anglican – (Henry VIII, Elizabeth I and their churchmen) - England

## Countries that remained Roman Catholic:

Italy, Spain, Portugal, France, Ireland, Austria, Poland.

## Countries of the Orthodox Faith:

### *Greek Orthodox*

Greece, Macedonia and parts of the Balkan area.

### *Russian Orthodox*

Russia and the Eastern Baltic lands.

## Post-Reformation Europe:

European civilisation and learning advanced tremendously due to the Renaissance. Religious wars such as the Thirty Years War were devastating and set it back. The Peace of Westphalia of 1648 ended religious wars in continental Europe. State churches were the norm in post-reformation Europe. The main framework of modern Europe had been established. Some change would come in the course of the Napoleonic war, the Franco-Prussian War, the Great War, the Second World War and the Cold War. Nevertheless, the European nations that entered into the colonisation of the world from the 16th to the 19th centuries would take those religions with them into their colonies.

## Reflections on the Reformation in Scotland

The Reformation took hold in Scotland absolutely, completely and entirely. Anything that hits a nation with such gigantic force makes a huge impact that is difficult to over-estimate. Religion was of crucial importance in national life and in the lives of the people. Imagine what those times and succeeding times must have been like.

Stories would have been told and events recounted over and over. Parents would tell their children and their children's children. Grandparents would be involved. With three or four generations involved in the telling of the story, this would encompass the best part of a hundred years. The people loved their national religion. The old Roman system was so corrupt as to disgust the people. The new reformed faith was full of energy and good intent. To them the organisation of the church mattered. They loved having a parish church, a congregation in the community. They loved the Presbyterian system where elders they knew and trusted took care of affairs that were vital to them. They loved the ministers who devoted all their time and energy to the church. They were happy to send them once a year to the General Assembly where the rules were made in Scotland for Scotland. Edinburgh was better than Rome. The people truly believed they were serving God aright and their service was acceptable to Him. Like ripples from a stone thrown into a pond, the ripples of the Reformation come down to us in the pond of time. From 1560 to 1960 is four hundred years - about 14 generations, both of these being nice Biblical numbers! It is only now that the ripples are dying away. Generations prior to 1960 kept the Protestant faith. Generations since have turned their back on the national church. As a boy growing up in Edinburgh, the writer remembers generations of families going to church, 'the kirk' on Sundays. Aunts, uncles, grandparents, cousins - all hurried on a Sunday morning to turn out in 'Sunday best' for church services. Now, that aspect of the life of the nation has disappeared. However, the strength with which it held the nation and the length of time it lasted bear testimony to its enormous force.

# THE RADICAL REFORMATION

## The 16th Century Anabaptist Movement

Activity to reform and guard the church against apostasy has been part of Christendom since the time of the first falling away. Later, some of the groups that acted to counter apostasy were given specific names. The story of many of these movements is shrouded in the mists of time and largely unknown. Groups such as the Catharists made their impact in Europe as far back as the 11th century. The Arnoldians succeeded the Cathari ("Pure Ones") and the Humiliati ("Humble Ones"). Arnold of Brescia was born about the year 1100 in Italy and educated in Paris. Expelled from Italy, he lived in Zurich before dying a martyr's death in Rome. After this, the Petrobrusians, appeared (followers of Peter of Bruys) and the Waldensians (followers of Peter Waldo of Lyons). Waldo died in Bohemia. The movement, which dates from the mid 12th century, was succeeded by the Albigenses (named from the town of Albi in southern France), in the early 13th century. Following this, the Papacy set up the Inquisition to deal with heresy. Once it had run its terrible course, reform movements arose once more. Sixteenth century Europe offered a different situation for reformers. Back in the 12th and 13th centuries, the Roman Catholic Church dominated Europe and some of the most powerful Popes in history ruled. The 16th century was still a dangerous and a brutal time. However, changes had taken place that loosened the grip of the Papacy. The Renaissance brought about many things, not least of which was the rebirth of learning in terms of education and science, as well as advances in technology like the invention of the printing press. Emerging nationalism in many nations meant that both leaders and people felt less allegiance to the Pope. Nevertheless, it was still a time of tumult and movements such as the Anabaptists were born in stormy times. The nineteenth century Restoration Movement that produced modern Churches of Christ has little to connect it to these earlier movements. This writer is not of the persuasion that needs to trace our ecclesiastical heritage through every age back to apostolic times. It is enough that Jesus said with regard to his church that 'the gates of Hades would not prevail against it' (Matthew 16:18). The Lord's church is never going to die out from this earth. We have God's word on that. Churches of Christ today are based on the authority of the New Testament. Indeed, we had better be sure that we are among the spiritual descendents of the apostolic faith. Those blessings are to be found in the Word of God but having said that, men and women who took their stand for truth have also blessed our lives. The Brethren or Anabaptist movement of the sixteenth century set forth doctrines and preached principles that we subscribe to today for the simple reason that they are Biblical. The world of those sixteenth century Anabaptists was very different to our world and even the world of our nineteenth century Restoration forefathers. The Anabaptist search for truth has blessed those who would follow the same quest in succeeding centuries.

Europe was in the midst of tempestuous times and swift change. Onto this stage stepped an Augustinian monk, Martin Luther. Deep-seated grievances against his church were leading him away from the Roman Catholic fold. Matters came to a head on October 31 1517 when he nailed his famous 95 theses to the door of the church building in Wittenberg, Germany. Straight away, the flame of the Reformation was burning around Augsburg in Southern Germany. From there it spread to Zurich, Switzerland where by 1518, Huldreich Zwingli was preaching the reformed faith. By 1521, the followers of the new reformation broke with the Roman Catholic Church. All of this occurred in a matter of just four years. In that same year, 1521, Thomas Munzer was forced to leave Saxony (Eastern Germany around Dresden, Leipzig and Zwickau) because of his unorthodox religious views. He headed for Zurich, Switzerland. There by the following year, 1522, he found zealous groups of younger people who supported the Reformation, meeting in groups for Bible study and prayer. Reformation fervour was sweeping through the canton. Leading the reformers were Conrad Grebel (1498-1526) and Felix Manz (1498-1527). They wanted a more radical reform movement than that being led by Zwingli. Younger people said that Luther and Zwingli were not going far enough with reform. In 1524, these radical reformers broke with Zwingli and his newly established Reformed Church. George Jacob (1491-1529) of Coire, named Blaurock because of his blue cloak, joined them. He became the great evangelist of the movement. One area in which they disagreed with Zwingli was baptism. The Reformed churches of Luther and Zwingli still maintained infant baptism by sprinkling. The Grebel-Manz movement soon came to see that according to Scripture baptism was for adults and by immersion ('believer's baptism.') On the 21st of January 1525, just seven years after the beginning of the Reformation, the first of these radical reformers was immersed. Grebel immersed Blaurock and was himself immersed along with six others in the River Sitter near St Gall. This small group then gathered in the home of Felix Manz at Zollikon, on the lakeshore just outside Zurich to celebrate the Lord's Supper in the bread and the fruit of the vine. Zwingli was concerned at this. Indeed, Zwingli and Luther along with their followers opposed them, calling them Anabaptists, meaning baptised again. They referred to themselves simply as Brethren. By the end of that year, 1525, their views had permeated the Zurich area. Grebel tried to influence Zwingli who tolerated him but increasingly regarded him and his followers as dangerous radicals. Grebel and Manz appealed to the citizens of Zurich but its citizenry was represented by a council of 200 men who exercised political and ecclesiastical power. Zwingli preferred to work through this system rather than putting power directly into the hands of the people. Rejected by Zwingli, Grebel turned to Pastor Wilhelm Reublin of Zollikon and Louis Hertzer. Together they formed a congregation within the larger congregation of the Gross Munster, the cathedral church of Zurich. Admittance into the group was by the new baptism of true believers and not infant baptism, which they declared to be a horrible abomination invented by Pope Nicholas II. The Zurich council held a public discussion. These 'disputations' could last for days. The Anabaptists refused to yield. The council passed harsh laws against then. Some were imprisoned. Foreigners were banished. They maintained their testimony - "Not by words alone but with our blood are we ready to bear testimony to the truth of our cause." They saw this as a struggle between the Word of God and the word of Zwingli.

The practice of immersion rather than sprinkling or pouring was confirmed from that time with the baptism of a former monk, Wolfgang Ulimann in the River Rhine at Schaffhausen in February 1525. Ulimann joined in the preaching of the Gospel and over 500 were immersed in the River Sitter. They formed a congregation at St Galen. Along with Blaurock, Conrad Grebel went to his home town of Grunningen to evangelise and many obeyed the Gospel message. However, they were arrested and given long prison sentences. This so weakened Grebel's health that, after escaping from prison, he fell victim to the plague and died in 1526 at the age of 28. Manz too suffered persecution and served many prison sentences. At the beginning of the next year, 1527, he was arrested, tried and convicted. With Zwingli's approval, the court sentenced him to death by drowning. On the 5th of January, bearing witness to the Gospel of Christ, he went to the riverside. There he was tied up and thrown into the River Limmat. The first leaders were dead but the movement survived because it stood upon the Word of God. Men are easily killed, ideas are more difficult to kill but 'the Word of the Lord endures forever' (I Peter 1:25).

By 1527, Anabaptists had arrived in Berne. They clamoured for reform but it was not easy, especially in such a short time. To undo wrongs and correct beliefs that had been entrenched for a thousand years was difficult. By 1528, the movement was strong in southern Germany, especially around Strasburg and Augsburg. However, emotional excesses came in as they claimed the Holy Spirit. One of the worst examples of this was the case of Thomas Schucker. On the 16th of February 1526, supposedly under the influence of the Holy Spirit, Thomas dispatched his brother Leonard on to glory, beheading him 'in the name of God' as he knelt before him. Thomas was executed later that day. Such incidents tarnished and hindered the movement but, especially around Zurich, it continued to grow. After questioning the reformers on the practice of infant baptism, the radicals then questioned the practice of tithing. Tithing provided support for churches and schools, the very things that drove the reformation. Zwingli thought they were going too far and drew the line at that point. The Anabaptists pressed on. They refused to recognise civil authority, which they saw as pagan and not of God. They taught that Christians could not hold public office or bear arms. They had now become too great a threat to the church and the state. In these early years church and state operated together to give mutual support in their stand against Roman Catholicism. Now the Anabaptists had questioned baptism by which children born within the state are also added to the church. They questioned tithing, a practice whereby both church and state derived much income. They questioned public office and armed service whereby the state maintains order and protects itself. They were seen as anarchists threatening the order of society and society rose up to reject what it saw as destructive elements. Manz had been drowned in January 1527. Blaurock was scourged with rods in Zurich and fled to the Tyrol where he was caught and burned by Roman Catholics in 1529. The same year, the Diet of Speier decreed that Anabaptists should be put to death. Two thousand perished immediately and untold thousands later. The means of execution were horrible - they were tied and drowned and they were burned alive. In 1530 Luther urged, "The use of the sword against them by right of law" but still the movement survived and spread. It travelled down the River Rhine, the major line of communication at the time, to the area known as the Palatinate (western Germany around Heidelberg). Further north, it took root in northern Germany and Holland. It spread to Moravia, a province between the towns of Brno and Ostrava and Bohemia, which centres on Prague in the present day Czech Republic. In 1534, non-pacifist Anabaptists took Munster in Germany for their own city. They were repelled by force and another wave of persecution began against Anabaptists of all shades. As the movement fell into the hands of extreme elements, it began to fragment. A Roman Catholic priest who became part of the movement in Holland in

1536 saved it. His name was Menno Simons (1496-1561). His followers came to be known as Mennonites. Simons exerted a steady hand at a time when the movement needed stability. Balthaser Hubmeier (1480-1528) of Ingolstadt (north of Munich in Bavaria) did the same in Bohemia, now part of the Czech Republic centred on Prague, the city where John Huss worked in earlier years.

With the death of Grebel and Manz and the banishment of Blaurock, the Anabaptist Movement in Switzerland suffered a severe blow from which it never really recovered. Anabaptists were persecuted from both sides, Roman Catholic and Reformed. Councils in the Swiss cantons persecuted Anabaptists with fines and imprisonment and drove them out or killed them. These Swiss brethren were scattered to southern Germany, Moravia in the present-day Czech Republic and on to Poland, northern Germany and the Netherlands.

Across Europe, the Anabaptist movement or the Church of the Brethren, to give it its proper name, went on to over a century of peace and prosperity. It more than just survived, it thrived. By the 1690's the movement was widespread but it had grown slack in its discipline. Church discipline was very much an issue when Jakob Ammann, a Swiss Mennonite, advocated the practice of true discipline or as they referred to it, 'shunning.' His followers came to be known as the Amish. The followers of Jacob Hutter, who had shepherded the Brethren in Moravia, came to be known as Hutterites. The followers of Menno Simons were from the first known as Mennonites. Later all these groups would experience another wave of persecution in eighteenth century Europe. It was not as severe or barbaric as the sixteenth century persecution and took the form of non-recognition, discrimination and social exclusion. At that time, many of them emigrated from Europe to the New World. The Anabaptist witness continues today in the Mennonite, Amish and Hutterite churches. The Mennonites went throughout the USA. The Amish concentrated on the northeastern states of the USA. The Hutterites focused on Canada. These groups have died out in Europe but they continue to thrive in North America. The Mennonite Historical Library is at Goshen College in Indianapolis, Indiana.

The reader will have noticed points concerning doctrine, which are still an issue today in Churches of Christ. Christians today can identify with Anabaptist thought. Of course, it follows that if they went down the road of Scripture we must follow in the same way. We owe much to these early reformers. Those who came out of the fray went on to establish a quiet existence in rural America where they were free to follow their own conscience. The first generations fought for their beliefs at a time when such a fight was hard and dangerous in the extreme. Persecution unto death was still a reality and that came upon many thousands of them. They willingly gave their life for their faith. The Anabaptist movement survived but Protestant Reformed churches claimed northern Europe. Two hundred and fifty years later another restoration movement came along in the nineteenth century. The political and social climate in which it grew was less harsh and more tolerant than those early Brethren experienced. Purity of church was what mattered to those early reformers. To later reformers purity of doctrine would be paramount. The restoration movement they established has direct links with churches of Christ today. We shall take up that story later but here we honour those men and women of the sixteenth century who gave their lives for the faith. It is appropriate at this point to give a brief sketch of the life of Radical Reformation leaders.

## Conrad Grebel (1498-1526)

Grebel was born into a wealthy family in Gruningen, just East of Zurich. He studied classics at the University of Vienna under humanist scholars. He never completed his studies due to living a somewhat wild life. Prospective studies in Paris fell through and he returned home in 1520. In Zurich, he began to study theology and Greek with Zwingli. His 'conversion' came in 1522. However, in 1524 he split with Zwingli over the question of infant baptism. It was Grebel who initiated the immersions on that historic evening in January 1525. The next month he immersed Ulimann into Christ. Later, the authorities made the act of performing immersion a crime punishable by death. By that time, Grebel was the subject of severe persecution and suffered a time in prison. This weakened his health, which was never particularly strong, and he succumbed to the plague sometime later, probably in August 1526. His manuscript on baptism was published in 1527. He never attained the age of 30 and his ministry lasted less than two years but his courage and leadership made a tremendous stamp on his times and he left a great heritage for others.

## Felix Manz (1498-1527)

Manz was a citizen of Zurich, the son of a Roman Catholic Canon. He began as a Roman Catholic priest but soon joined the Reformation led by Zwingli. He was fluent in Biblical languages, a good scholar and a very able preacher. Zwingli continued to favour a state church. Manz believed in the all-sufficiency of Scripture and did not see any basis for a connection between church and state. Along with

Grebel, he became one of the leaders in the Anabaptist movement. He was often imprisoned for his beliefs and ultimately he was put to death by drowning on the 5th of January 1527 at 29 years of age. The death sentence read that, "Manz shall be delivered to the executioner, who shall tie his hands, put him into a boat, take him to the lower hut, there strip his bound hands down over his knees, place a stick between his knees and arms and thus push him into the water and let him perish in the water." According to the sentence, Manz was taken from the Wellenberg prison to the bank of the River Limmat. All along the way, he witnessed to the faith and praised God that he would die for the truth. His mother's voice was heard encouraging him to remain true to Christ. Just below the Rathaus (the town council hall), he was put in the boat and taken to the fisherman's hut in the middle of the river. As he was being bound, he sang out "Into Thy hands, O Lord, I commend my spirit." With that, he was cast into the water. Berhard Wyss, the Zurich chronicler recorded that it was 3 pm on Saturday, 5th January 1527. He was the first martyr to die according to the law against re-baptising, which had come into force the previous year.

## George Blaurock (1491-1529)

Blaurock was born near Chur in Graubunden canton. His family name was Jacob but he became known as Blaurock after the blue coat he wore. He was educated at the University of Leipzig and became a Roman Catholic priest. However, by the time he returned home he was committed to the Reformation and quickly identified with Grebel and Manz in the Anabaptist cause. Of tall and robust stature, he was known as the Hercules of the Anabaptist movement because of the scope and intensity of his labours. He was arrested and thrown in jail in Zurich on the day Manz was drowned. He only escaped death because he was not a native of Zurich and the Council had no jurisdiction over those born outside Zurich. From Zurich, he went to Berne and throughout all the Swiss cantons preaching the Gospel, baptising believers and forming congregations. He did the same throughout Austria. In 1529, the Roman Catholic authorities in Innsbruck arrested him. He was tortured and burned at the stake in Gufidaun.

## Wilhelm Reublin

Reublin was born in Rottenberg and educated at the University of Freiberg. He ministered as a Roman Catholic priest in Basle preaching to congregations of over 4,000. He replaced a relic with a copy of the Bible and after a sharp dispute, he was banished and moved to Zurich in 1522. There he met Zwingli and became a reformer. He settled at Wytikon as the preacher for Zollikon. He began to preach against infant baptism in 1524 and took part in the first 'Disputation' with Zwingli in January 1525. He was expelled from the city and moved to Schaffhausen as a confirmed Anabaptist. It was there, in the spring of 1525, that he immersed Hubmaier into Christ along with 60 other believers. In 1528, he was expelled from Schaffhausen and moved to Strasburg. He then moved to Moravia and associated with the Hutterite communities, gathering a congregation at Eslingen. Later he returned to live in Rottenberg, Zurich and Basle.

## Thomas Muntzer (1488-1525)

Muntzer was born in Stolberg, near Halle in Saxony. He was a charismatic character and belonged to the spiritist group known as the Zwickau Prophets. He remained within the

Lutheran fold although he had links with the Anabaptists. For instance he was part of the Munster uprising. He was arrested after the Battle of Mulhausen and although he recanted and reverted to Roman Catholicism, he was put to death, being beheaded in 1525.

## Johannes (Hans) Denck (1500-1527)

Denck was born in upper Bavaria and educated in classics at the University of Ingolstadt. He joined the Erasmus school of scholars in Basle. He was converted and baptised by Hubmaier at Augsburg in 1526. Like many Anabaptists he was a pacifist and firmly committed to 'the more excellent way' (I Corinthians 12:31). Like most Anabaptists, he was hounded out of Augsburg by persecution and moved to join Grebel and Manz in Zurich and then St Galen. In 1527, over a thousand Brethren gathered regularly for worship in Augsburg.

## Michael Sattler (1490-1527)

Sattler was born in Stauffen, near Freiburg, Germany in 1490. His monastic education taught him Hebrew and Greek. His own Bible study led him to leave the Roman Catholic Church and join with Luther. Persecution led him to Zurich where he was converted by the preaching of Wilhelm Reublin. He became an itinerant preacher. At an Anabaptist conference in Schleitheim, near Schaffhausen, he wrote what is known as the 'Schleitheim Confession of Faith.' This became the standard statement of faith for sixteenth century Anabaptists. After the conference, he was arrested. On the 15th of May 1527, a show-trial was convened in Rottenberg to try Sattler for heresy. He was executed on May 20th in the manner prescribed by the court. Wilhelm Reublin recorded the story. The sentence ordered Sattler to be committed to the executioner, "who shall cut out his tongue, then forge him to a wagon and then, with glowing tongs, twice tear pieces of flesh from his body; then on the way to the place of execution, five times more to repeat the same and then burn his body to powder as an arch-heretic." In the market place and at the site of his execution, still able to speak and unshakeable in his faith, Sattler prayed for his persecutors. After being bound to a ladder with ropes and pushed into the fire, he admonished the people, the judges and the mayor to repent and be converted. Then he prayed, "Almighty, eternal God, thou art the way and the truth: because I have not been shown to be in error, I will with thy help to this day testify to the truth and seal it with my blood." As soon as the ropes on his wrists burned through, Sattler raised the two forefingers of his hands giving the promised signal to the brethren that a martyr's death was bearable. Then the assembled crowd heard the words coming from his seared lips, "Father, I commend my spirit into thy hands." After every attempt to secure a recantation from Sattler's faithful wife had failed, she was drowned eight days later in the River Neckar.

## Johannes (Hans) Hut (1495-1527)

Hut was born near Erfurt in mid-Germany. He had little formal education being a bookbinder and bookseller by trade. He was immersed into Christ by Denck in 1526. He became a fiery preacher working mainly in Austria where the number of converts to Anabaptist views was remarkable. Equally extra-ordinary were the numbers imprisoned, tortured and killed. Hut became one of them after the 'Martyr's Synod' at Augsburg in August 1527.

## Balthasar Hubmaier (1486-1528)

Hubmaier was born near Augsburg in Bavaria. He was the most brilliant theologian of the Radical Reformation educated at the Universities of Freiburg and Augsburg. At 19 years of age, he was lecturing in Old and New Testament. At 23, he was a Professor of Theology and in 1510, he was elected as Rector of Augsburg University. He received his priestly orders from the Bishop of Constance. He then went to Ingolstadt University and served as the preacher for the city's largest congregation. Later he moved to preach at Regensburg. He remained a loyal Roman Catholic through all of this. Disgusted by the excesses of his church he moved to Waldshut where he became a Lutheran. However, he favoured Zwingli's theology rather than Luther's. Zwingli and Hubmaier even agreed that baptising infants was not Biblical, though Zwingli later reneged on this. Forced to flee from Waldshut by the Austrian Roman Catholic authorities, he escaped to Schaffhausen. From 1525, he came closer and closer to Grebel's position and he was immersed into Christ by Wilhelm Reublin. Forced to flee once more, he moved throughout Switzerland, Southern Germany and the Austrian Tyrol. At Nikolsberg, between Vienna and Brno in Moldavia, a city of 12,000 Anabaptists, he was responsible for over 2,000 baptisms. Hubmaier was an outstanding scholar and student of the Bible. His output in terms of debates, tracts and books was second to none. In the summer of 1527, he was arrested, imprisoned and tortured in Vienna. On the 10th of March 1528, he was burned at the stake. His faithful wife was drowned in the River Danube three days later.

## Jacob Hutter (c.1490-1536)

Hutter was born in the Austrian Tyrol. He became an Anabaptist and led the Brethren in Moravia. The groups he worked with came to be known as Hutterite communities. They organised themselves, set up schools for their children, worked and worshipped together and were completely independent. By 1575, they had a membership of around 30,000. Hutter was caught, tortured and burned at the stake on the 25th of February 1536.

## Melchior Hoffman (1495-1543)

Hoffman brought Anabaptist teaching to the Netherlands. He was a furrier by trade and a follower of Luther. However, on hearing Anabaptist preaching he was immersed into Christ at Strasburg in 1530. He preached throughout the Netherlands and North Germany, mainly in Amsterdam, Leeuwarden and Emden. Like Munzer, he was distinctly spiritist in his interpretation of Scripture was thus outside of Biblical Anabaptism as preached by Hubmaier and mainstream Anabaptists. On hearing a prophecy that he would be imprisoned and that six months later Christ would return, he sought imprisonment and the authorities in Strasburg duly obliged. He was imprisoned in 1533. Ten years later, still in prison, he died.

## Pilgram Marpeck (1495-1556)

Marpeck was born in Rattenberg in the Austrian Tyrol. He graduated from university as a civil engineer. As a city official, he was supposed to suppress the Anabaptists but instead, he became an Anabaptist himself. The year was 1527. This cost him his job and he moved to Strasburg in 1528. He became a leader of the Anabaptists after

Reublin left. In Strasburg, he became popular with the city authorities due to his civil engineering skills. He was a great debater and writer. Many of his writings were published, including a confession of faith along with works on baptism and the Lord's Supper. He published his own concordance. He debated with the Lutheran reformer, Martin Bucer. That led to his expulsion from Strasburg and he went to Augsburg where he also served as city engineer. He died in that office in December 1556. His contribution in terms of scholarship and writing was immense.

## Peter Reidemann (1506-1556)

Riedemann was born in Hirschberg in Silesia and was a cobbler by trade. He served three years in prison for his Anabaptist sympathies. Once released in 1532 he began an intensive and powerful period of labour as a Hutterite missionary. He was again imprisoned in Nurnberg in 1537. After his release, he preached in Hesse but was again imprisoned in Marburg and then moved to the Castle of Wolkersdorf. As Luther did when deprived of liberty, he wrote. His 'Confession' became a classic of Anabaptist literature. Once freed, he returned to Moravia in 1542 and led the Brethren there. He was pre-eminent among second generation Anabaptists. He died in Moravia in 1556.

## Menno Simons (1496-1561)

Simons was born in Witmarsum in Holland. He was educated and ordained to the Roman Catholic priesthood at the University of Utrecht in 1524. Two things had a big impact on him. First, he witnessed the beheading of an Anabaptist for being 'twice baptised.' Second, the slaughter of 300 Anabaptists at Bolsward including his own brother horrified him. His own study of the New Testament led him to the faith and immersion into Christ. In January 1536, he resigned his living and left the Roman Catholic Church. He was immersed into Christ by Obbe Philips. He wanted to preach in Groningen but a price of 100 Gulden had been put on his head and he was forced to become an itinerant preacher throughout Germany and Denmark. He founded congregations everywhere he went. He wrote voluminously. After the Munster tragedy, he saved the Anabaptist Movement in northern Europe from disintegrating. He was a careful scholar and gave the church a sound, systematic theology. He returned to his native land settling in Holstein where he died. His lifelong ministry made a lasting impression and his followers are still popularly known as Mennonites to this day.

## EARLY CHURCHES OF CHRIST IN ENGLAND

### Falsely called Anabaptists

Ideas often travel further and faster than we think. National borders cannot contain them. Kings exercise authority to control the life and thinking of their subjects. They like to be in control. Authorities dislike independent thought because it cannot be controlled. Generally and particularly at the times under consideration, they see religious freedom as anarchy and a challenge to their position. True religion recognises proper authority, namely God's anointed, the Christ and his appointed and then kings and all those in positions of authority.

The church of the early Britons, which we call the Celtic church, may have been fairly close to the church of apostolic times. With the imposition of the Roman Catholic system by Augustine in the 7th century, Britain became Roman

Catholic. There is evidence that the ideas of the Waldensians reached Britain. Followers of the Waldensian faith were persecuted, tortured and branded as heretics. People were forbidden to aid them and lacking shelter, food and clothing, they wandered the countryside until they died. They were known as 'Bible Men' and as they wandered, they gave themselves to teaching and preaching the Bible. There are records of groups in Kent and East Anglia. After this, John Wycliffe emerged and his followers were known as the Lollards. Like their antecedents, the Waldenses, the Lollards formed small independent groups that existed in various places in England from the 12th to the 17th centuries. Persecuted by the Roman Catholic Church and the authorities, from the Crown through Parliament right down to town councils and local magistrates, these groups had to remain almost secret societies. They existed as underground groups, always persecuted, always outside the law and ready to flee at a moment's notice. Gradually times changed. Bibles became available. Preaching became popular. Toleration increased little by little. Gradually non-conformist groups grew in number and began to emerge as a force to be reckoned with in society even though the way was still very difficult for them.

Puritans, Separatists and Anabaptists were all classified as non-conformists or dissenters. In the 16th and 17th centuries not to conform or the converse, to dissent, was unacceptable, against the law and ultimately punishable by death. Puritans saw the Church of England as so corrupt that they wanted to purify it. However, they stayed within the Anglican Communion. Separatists on the other hand saw the Church of England as so corrupt that they wanted no part of it and separated themselves from it. They left the

Church of England to establish independent congregations of their own.

England had been warned about Anabaptists. In 1531, William Barlow described it as the 'third faction' of the Reformation. Presumably, the other two were the Lutheran and the Reformed Churches. About this time, the first Dutch Anabaptists refugees came to England. By 1534, they were preaching their faith. In 1535, twenty-five of them were arrested in London. Fourteen of the group were burned at the stake. They continued to preach and publish tracts. In 1538, one of their leaders, Jan Matthijsz, was burned at Smithfield. The same fate befell another, Jan Boucher, in 1550.

Several Church of England ministers including John Bale of Colchester adopted some Anabaptist views. Henry Hart, the leader of a dissenter group in Kent, supported Anabaptist views and published tracts in defence of these views in 1548. In fact, Hart and his fellow non-conformists were referred to as Anabaptists. They made such an impression on the religious world that in 1560 John Knox, leader of the Reformation in Scotland, felt the need to publish a book refuting Anabaptist teaching. In 1575, large groups of Anabaptists were arrested in London and Ely and imprisoned.

In the 16th century, Anabaptists quickly took over the mantle of the Lollards as radical reformers. However, Anabaptist was not a name the English took to nor did the Anabaptists use it of themselves. Native English groups, especially the Separatists, soon assimilated Anabaptist views. Although Anabaptists were still to be found in the middle of the 17th century, the concepts of Anabaptism were to spread out and would be found among other groups. The most important creed of the Church of England, the 42 Articles of 1553, contained many articles against Anabaptism.

Puritans and Separatists began to appear in England around 1550. Two of the earliest groups, about 60 persons in all, were in Bocking in Essex and Faversham in Kent. They held much Anabaptist theology. Their leaders were arrested in 1551. Henry Hart was one of them and he was imprisoned. Another, Humphrey Middleton, was burned at the stake. Two other non-conformist congregations surfaced in London. One was a Puritan group, the Plumber's Hall congregation. After being arrested, their leader, William Bonham, along with twenty-four members were released from Brydwell prison in 1569 having promised to cease from unorthodox practices. The other was a Separatist group led by Richard Fitz, known as the Privy Church of London. Two of the leaders, Fitz himself and Thomas Bowlande, were put to death. Some others may have been killed or at least imprisoned. By 1571, the congregation had been stamped out and the members scattered. Indeed many prisons must have played host to various and numerous non-conformists, Separatist, Anabaptists and other. It would be interesting to know what ideas were shared and doctrines discussed in the prison cells of England.

Ten years later, in 1581, Robert Browne and Robert Harrison formed a Separatist congregation in Norwich. Persecution forced the group to flee to Holland in 1581. After Browne another Separatist, John Penry came to the fore. Penry was Welsh and came to be one of the first notable ministers of an Independent or Congregational church. Persecution in England forced him to flee to Scotland in 1589 but it was no easier and he only remained there for a short time before returning to England. There he was arrested and sentenced to death by hanging at Tyburn in 1593.

Henry Barrowe, a lawyer, was another Separatist leader in London in the 1590's. He was thoroughly Anabaptist in doctrine except for baptism itself. His followers, called Barrowists, did not practice infant baptism but neither did they practice believer's baptism. Barrowe was assisted by a clergyman, John Greenwood. Barrowe and Greenwood were arrested for refusing to recognise the supremacy of the Queen in religion. Both were sentenced to death by hanging in 1593. After this, their followers fled to take refuge at Campen in Holland. A year later, some of this group became Anabaptists. The year 1594 therefore marks the formation of the first English Anabaptist congregation at Campen. A second English Anabaptist congregation was formed at Naarden. Thomas Mitchell returned to Norwich to preach his new Anabaptist faith. It is possible he influenced John Smyth concerning believer's baptism. In the meantime, Francis Johnson (1562-1618), a Puritan minister, changed over to become a Separatist. He was imprisoned but on his release in 1597, he fled to Holland. There he became the leader of the Barrowists.

In 1602, John Smyth assisted by William Brewster formed a Separatist congregation at Gainsborough. A second was formed by Brewster and John Robinson at Scrooby. Both congregations suffered persecution and both fled to Holland in 1607. The Gainsborough group settled in Amsterdam and the Scrooby group in Leiden. In Amsterdam, Smyth encountered Mennonites and through their influence and his own study of the Bible, he rejected infant baptism. In 1608, he 'baptised' himself and other adults by pouring. Smyth died in 1612 and the mantle of leadership fell on Thomas Helwys and John Murton. They led most of the Amsterdam group back to London in 1612. It was this group that constituted what history recognises as the first Baptist congregation in England. Because they were Arminian in theology, they are referred to as General Baptists. Helwys is thought to have died in prison in 1616, the same year that Henry Jacob led most of the Leiden group back to London. They were Calvinistic in theology and in 1541 established the first Particular Baptist congregation in England. Like Separatist and other names, the name Anabaptist fell into disuse and the name Baptist became commonly applied to such groups because they continued to use the mode of baptism of the Anabaptists, namely immersion, which became the standard practice for all English Baptists.

A small group within the Leiden congregation led by Brewster decided to venture further a field. In 1620, they set sail in the ship Mayflower and landed at Plymouth Rock, Massachusetts. History knows them as 'the Pilgrim Fathers.' They had been preceded by the first English colonists 13 years earlier. Anglicans established the first English colony in Jamestown, Virginia in 1607. By 1628, continual emigration began. Massachusetts was established by Royal Charter in 1628 and Connecticut in 1636. Ministers went with their flocks. Among the more prominent, John Winthrop (1588-1649), John Cotton (1584-1652) and Richard Mather (1596-1669) settled in Plymouth, Boston and Dorchester, Massachusetts. Thomas Hooker (1586-1647) and John Davenport (1597-1670) settled in Hartford and New Haven, Connecticut. They were all zealous Anglicans, indeed Puritans. From 1630 to 1640, at least 20,000 Puritans came to New England. Not all the leaders who came were established churchmen however. Some were non-conformists. Roger Williams (1599-1689) established the Rhode Island colony in 1636 and founded the first Baptist congregation in America in 1639. Dutch Mennonites were in New Amsterdam (New

York) as early as 1643. They were referred to as Menists. They had no minister of their own and being few in number, they worshipped with German Anabaptists. Both groups would turn to the faith of the Quakers. By the close of the 17th century, the Quakers were protesting against slavery and teaching the Native American Indians.

Religious intolerance travelled with the immigrants from the old world to the new world. In 1644, Massachusetts passed an act to banish all Baptists from the state. Between 1656 and 1660, four Quakers were hanged in Boston. Only Pennsylvania, granted to William Penn in 1681, modelled the kind of freedom that would eventually come in with the Constitution, which promised 'liberty and justice for all.' Indeed Pennsylvania was an interesting mix with Quakers from England, Baptists from Wales, Presbyterians from Scotland and Mennonites and Dunkards from Holland and Germany. How they did not tear one another apart, we have no idea other than the fact that they formed a majority of minorities and a persecuted one at that. All these groups had experienced severe persecution and they were now prepared to extend some religious toleration. Some of the leaders from those times were:

## John Smyth (1567-1612)

Smyth was educated at the University of Cambridge and ordained as a priest in the Church of England in 1594, the same year the first English Anabaptist congregation was formed in Holland. He ministered in Lincoln and Gainsborough. He was a Puritan but no Separatist. On being reprimanded by his bishop for exceeding his licensed powers, he spent several months studying the Scriptures. His conclusions led him to leave the Church of England and he began an Independent congregation in Gainsborough. Persecution under King James I grew more severe and some of the members of the congregation were imprisoned in York Castle. In 1608, the rest fled to Amsterdam. Francis Johnson's congregation had been meeting there since 1597 and of course, there were many Dutch Mennonite congregations. As 1608 gave way to 1609 Smith was baptised, then Helwys, followed by the rest of the congregation. There is no doubt Smyth was influenced by Anabaptist teaching but above all, he took his stand on the New Testament and the teaching of Christ and the apostles. He died in Holland in 1612.

### Thomas Helwys (c.1550-1616)

Helwys was born near Northampton and was educated in law at Gray's Inn, London. At first, he worked with Smyth but later the two men divided. Smyth embraced Mennonite views quickly and extensively. Helwys was slower to come to the same position. Their followers split in 1610. Helwys then decided it was wrong to flee from persecution and led his followers back to England in 1612 where they formed a congregation at Spittalfields, London. This was the first Baptist congregation in England. Helwys produced many tracts in defence of his theological stance. He even wrote a book addressed to King James, 'The Mystery of Iniquity.' In it, he asserted that the King had no right before God to rule the church. For this, he was arrested and put in Newgate Prison where he died in 1616.

### Robert Browne (c.1550 - 1633)

Browne was borne in Tolethorpe, Rutlandshire. He was educated at the University of Cambridge and after graduating in 1572, he became a teacher. He held to Puritan views but he was also influenced by the Anabaptist views of

Thomas Cartwright. He spent some time in Middleburg, Holland. Back in England, he formed an Independent congregation at Norwich in 1581. This was the forerunner of the Congregational church. His followers were known as Brownists. Brown himself reverted to the Church of England in 1583 and he became a parish priest in 1591. He served in that capacity until his death in 1633.

## Confessions of Faith

Misunderstood and persecuted, these early reformers wrote down the main points of their beliefs in what they called 'Confessions of Faith.' Christians today are against confessions of faith, recognising them as human and not divine in origin. As such, they have a divisive rather than a unifying effect in Christendom. The early reformers were of the same mind. They placed no faith in these confessions, only in the God of the Scriptures. These confessions had no authority within their congregations. Why then, did they write them and what is their value? They were written for various reasons: to inform the ignorant, to correct misunderstanding, to appeal to the authorities for toleration, to affirm their loyalty to the crown and to publicise their faith. Let no one be misled or put off by the term 'confession of faith.' These were not creeds like the Nicene Creed of old, which were used to enforce orthodoxy. Rather, they were like the tracts that we use today and they were used in a similar way.

The first English confession appeared in 1611, written by John Smyth. It was subdivided into twenty articles or twenty short statements of what the congregation believed. Articles 8, 12, 14 & 15 are interesting. Article 8 said, "*That the grace of God through the finished redemption of Christ was to be prepared and offered to all without distinction.*" This was a charter for evangelism. People understood Calvin to say that grace was limited to the elect. Calvinistic churches continued with that doctrine. The church of which Smith was a part believed God's grace was open to all and that belief would be reflected in a passion for evangelism. Article 12 said, *"That the Church of Christ is a company of the faithful, baptised after confession of sin and of faith."* The only part of that which we might question is the idea of 'confession of sin.' We would rather say 'confession of Christ' believing it to be more accurate according to Scripture. Yet in one way, we do confess ourselves to be sinners in baptism. Why be baptised if not to wash away our sins? The principle is inherent in the process. Article 14 said, *"That baptism is the external sign of the remission of sins, of dying and being made alive and therefore does not belong to infants."* To that, we would say 'Amen.' We would also be careful not to carry it on to the point that many modern Baptists do, who say that baptism is the outward sign of an inward grace and not necessary to salvation. Their next step from there is to separate salvation and baptism saying a person is saved by grace and can be baptised later if they so wish to show that they have been saved. To do that is to wrest the Scripture to one's own destruction. Baptism always precedes salvation, albeit immediately and the forgiveness of sins always comes after baptism, also immediately. Article 15 said, *"That the Lord's Supper is the sign of the communion of Christ and of the faithful among themselves by faith and love."* It is an accurate statement with regard to the Lord's Supper. We would largely agree with all of this, not that we sit in judgement on their faith. We do not. Neither do we determine orthodoxy. Scripture does that. Nevertheless, it is interesting to look for common ties between these ancient movements and the Lord's church of today.

Also in 1611, a Confession by Thomas Helwys in twenty-seven articles became the first printed confession. Article 13 said, *"That everie Church is to receive in all their members by baptisme, upon the confession of their faith and sinnes, according to the primitive institucion."* Article 14 said, *"Baptisme in no wise apperteyneth to infants."* Article 22 said, *"That the officers of everie Church or congregacion are tied only to that particular congregacion. They cannot challenge by office anie auhthoitie in anie other congregacion whatsoever."* We would agree with all of these statements. It was Thomas Helwys who would lead the group back to England and establish a Church of Christ in Spittalfields, London in the year 1612.

In the 'Mystery of Iniquity' of 1612, Helwys said, *"The King is a mortall man and not God, therefore hath no power over the immortall soules of his subjects to make lawes for them and to set spiritual Lords over them."* In 1613 a 'Confession of English people living at Amsterdam' stated in Article 84, *"That the magistrate is not to meddle with religion, or matters of conscience, but to leave Christian religion free."* This was something that the 'Anabaptists' had maintained from the beginning in Zurich in 1521. In practice, it called for the separation of Church and State.

In 1644, a document was published in London that bore the title, *'Confession of Faith of those churches which are commonly though falsely called Anabaptists.'* A second impression was published in 1646. A fourth impression was published in Scotland at Leith, near Edinburgh in 1653. The Baptist Church refers to it as the first Baptist confession printed in Scotland. This is not so. Other than a similar sounding name, there is no ground to equate 'Anabaptist' with 'Baptist.' The 'Anabaptists' were not the forerunners of the Baptist Church of today. Other modern churches also have their roots in the 'Anabaptist' movement. To clear up a common misconception, these people were called 'Anabaptists' by those who were opposed to them. 'Anabaptist' means literally 'again baptised' or in better English 're-baptised.' They were so designated because their enemies thought they needlessly re-baptised people who had already been baptised as infants. They denied this vehemently saying that, *"Infant baptism is not Bible baptism. Indeed it is not baptism at all having no efficacy or authority according to Scripture."* The baptism they practiced was *"for believing and penitent adults and as such was the one true baptism of the New Testament."* 'Anabaptist' then was a general term that the state churches of the time used to define all 'Non-conformist' groups who practiced adult immersion. Those involved did not refer to themselves as 'Non-conformists' but as 'Brethren.' They did not refer to their congregations as 'Anabaptist' but as 'Churches of Christ.' These people were willing to give their life for their faith and many did. Surely, if for no other reason other than in recognition of their sacrifice, we should extend them the courtesy of referring to them as they would have preferred and as they referred to themselves.

Their main Confession, published in 1644 and republished in 1653, was titled *'Confession of faith of those churches which are commonly (though falsely) called Anabaptists.'* Numerous articles within the document are worthy of our consideration, especially Articles 36, 38, 39, 41, 43, & 46. Article 36 said, *"Every Church hath power given them from Christ for their well-being, to chuse amongst themselves meet persons for Elders and Deacons, being qualified according to the Word, as those which Christ hath appointed in His Testament, for the feeding, governing, serving and building up of His Church."* Article 38, *"Baptism is an Ordinance of the New Testament given by Christ, to be dispensed upon persons professing faith, or that are disciples; who upon profession of faith ought to be baptised, and after to partake of the Lord's Supper."* Article 39, *"The way and manner of dispensing this ordinance is by dipping or plunging the body under water, it being a sign, must answer the thing signified, which is, that interest the Saints have in the death, burial and resurrection of Christ."* Article 41, *"Christ hath likewise given power to His Church to receive in, and cast out, any member that deserves it, and this power is given to every congregation, and not to one particular person, either member or officer, but in relation to the whole body."* Article 43, *"Christ, for the keeping of the Church in holy and orderly communion, placeth some special men over the Church, who by their office are to govern, oversee, visit, watch, so likewise for the better keeping thereof, in all places by the members, He hath given authority and laid duty upon all to watch over one another."* Article 46, *"And although the particular congregations be distinct and several bodies, every one as a compact and knit city within itself; yet are they all to walk by the one rule of truth; so also they (by all means convenient) are to have the counsel and help one of another, if necessity require it, as members of one body, in the common faith, under Christ their head."*

How close is this to the practice of Churches of Christ in the 21st century? Yet this was three hundred and fifty years ago in the mid 17th century. It predates the Restoration Movement by one hundred and fifty years.

In 1651, a confession or tract was published entitled *'The faith and practice of thirty congregations.'* Article 47 said, *"That the baptisme which the Lord commanded ought to be known by everyone before they submit themselves, or obey it."* In other words, people were to be taught before they were baptised. This is entirely in harmony with Matthew 28:18-20. The paedo-baptist has yet to be seen who can teach the

Gospel and give instruction on baptism to a week old baby let alone communicate with them.

In 1656 *'Churches of Christ in the County of Somerset and near adjacent'* published a confession with this statement in Article 21. *"That in admitting of members it is the duty of the Church and its ministers, in faithfulness to God, that they be careful to receive none but such as do evident demonstration of the new birth."* Important principles we hold today are embodied in this statement. First, the new birth is essential in admitting individuals to the church. Second, the church is composed of those who have been born again. Therefore, all who are in the Church have been born again. If one has not been born again they, along with the apostate, are outside the Church, the body of Christ and therefore lost.

Another Confession, *'Set out by many of us who are falsely called Anabaptists'* appeared in July 1660. It was unique in that it was presented to the king, Charles II. Article 11 said, *"That the right and only way of gathering Churches is first to preach the Gospel, and then to baptise (that is in English to dip) such only as profess repentance toward God and faith towards our Lord Jesus Christ."* Article 24 stated, *"That it is the will of God that all men should have free liberty of their own consciences in matters of religion, without the least oppression or persecution."* In the first proposition, the Church had control of its own practice and indeed, it was already exercising such control. The second proposition was outside of their control and one that would not be granted. The father of Charles II, Charles I, had been executed in 1649 after the Civil War. Afterwards Oliver Cromwell became Lord Protector of the Kingdom during the time known as 'the Commonwealth' (c.1650-1660). After Cromwell's death, the monarchy was restored. Charles II who had fled into exile in France returned to London to be crowned king. Straight away, he had parliament pass strict laws to regulate religion. This was known as the Act of Conformity. Essentially, it said all churches and religious groups had to conform to the form of religion authorised and approved by the King. The King favoured a system where he controlled the church through Archbishops and Bishops. In practical terms, it said there is only room for one church in the realm, that being the Church of England, which had been established and granted favoured status under King Henry VIII in 1534. Churches of Christ appealed to the king against the Act of Conformity. Sadly, they along with all non-conformist groups were ignored and their religion was suppressed. Only the established Episcopal Church was allowed. Everyone in the kingdom paid the tithe, a tax that went to the state church. Non-conformists had to pay this tax and additionally had to bear very heavy fines for their non-conformism. However, in 1660 worse was to come. Throughout Britain, Non-conformist churches were persecuted. Puritans, Separatists and Anabaptists were outlawed. Quakers resisted and were pursued and slaughtered in their thousands. In Scotland, Presbyterians in their thousands signed the National Covenant of 1638, thereby vowing to defend their religion to the death and they were put to the test. These 'Covenanters' as they were called, fought and resisted the armies of Charles II for twenty-eight terrible years of absolute carnage and slaughter. The worst years were known as 'the Killing Times.' Many fell to the same fate as James Renwick who was the last martyr to be burned at the stake in the Grassmarket, Edinburgh in 1688. His death did at least signal the end of a time of fearsome and barbaric persecution.

In the meantime John Bunyan, an Independent and author of the classic Pilgrim's Progress, published a 'Confession of my faith' in 1672. In it he stated, *"I believe that Christ hath ordained water baptism and the supper of the Lord; they being to us representations of the death and resurrection of Christ."* He was imprisoned much and he wrote his classic of Christian literature while in Bedford gaol. 'Quaker' was another term that was given in a derogatory way. In 1650, George Fox, looking for a purer spiritual life than was generally found in the Church of England of his time, set up the Society of Friends. The title originated in Jesus' words "If you do what I say then you are my friends" (John 15:14). Persecuted under the Act of Conformity, Fox appeared in court at Derby in 1650 and had the temerity to tell the judge that he should "quake before the Lord." The judge knew of the meetings of Fox and his friends where they would shake with emotion. He said "You folk are the tremblers; you are the quakers" and sentenced Fox to six months in prison. Hence, the popular name for this group, 'the Quakers.' Fox and his Friends, especially the 'Valiant Sixty,' preachers, went everywhere preaching the Word. In a short time, the Quakers numbered 50,000. By 1700, there were 100,000. Their preaching was full of fire and brimstone and their lifestyle was austere in the extreme. In following their faith, they thought little of defying the state. Quakers were found in New England as early as 1660 and sent missionaries to the Indian tribes of North America. In the New World, there was often conflict between the Quakers and the Puritans, the two most radical groups.

In 1677, *'Elders and brethren of many congregations in London and the country'* stated in Article 29 of their Confession, *"Those who do actually profess repentance towards God, faith in, and obedience to our Lord Jesus are the only proper subjects of Baptism. Immersion is necessary to the due administration of this ordinance."*

In 1679, a statement appeared under the title, *'An Orthodox Creed.'* Article 30 said *"The marks by which she (a Church) is known to be the true spouse of Christ are these: Where the word of God is rightly preached, and the sacraments truly administered, according to Christ's institution, and the practice of the primitive Church; having discipline and government duly executed by ministers and pastors of God's appointing and the Church's election"*

Finally, in 1689, twenty-eight years of savage persecution ended. King Charles II died in 1685 and he was succeeded by James II, whose reign lasted only three years. Two things went against him. He came to the throne as a Roman Catholic in a Protestant land. He was even harsher than his predecessor was and very quickly established the tyrannical type of regime that had characterised the Stuart dynasty. This was based on the precept of 'the Divine Right of Kings.' Charles I went to his death rather than relinquish this principle. The people and parliament rose to resist James II and he fled to a life of exile in France. However, the daughter of James II, Mary, had married a Dutch Prince and a Protestant, William of Orange. She was the closest heir to the throne and parliament invited her and her husband to assume the throne of Great Britain as co-regents. This was the 'Glorious Revolution' of 1688. In France, a century later, the monarchy would be abolished quickly and brutally in the French Revolution resulting in the establishment of a republic. In Britain, the Glorious Revolution produced a gentler change to what the United Kingdom is today, a parliamentary democracy with the monarch as the head of state. Immediately after their accession in 1689, William and Mary had parliament pass the Act of Toleration. It allowed every individual the right to believe and practice their faith according to their own conscience. With the change came a new age of religious freedom which ushered in what is considered the modern era of Church History, the age in which we live today.

Very quickly under this new freedom, opportunity was taken to exercise and publish beliefs that had previously been banned.  Even at the time of proscription under the law of the land, those of 'Non-conformist' beliefs had carried on with the exercise of their faith.  In England under the term 'Anabaptist,' Churches of Christ had been constituted in London in 1612.  At the other extremity of England, in what is today referred to as the Lake District, the same thing occurred.  At Tottlebank, Cumbria in 1669, Churches of Christ were constituted.  A minute book still exists for four such congregations around Ulverston.  Today there is still a Church of Christ meeting in Ulverston.  In Scotland a man called John Glas, a minister of the Church of Scotland, committed himself to the process of reformation.  Based on his study of the Scriptures he abandoned the established church and took up independent principles.  He was deposed as a minister of the Kirk and his followers were given the name 'Glasites.'  Again, this was not a name he or his followers would have approved.  The last lines of the epitaph on his tombstone read, *"His character in the Churches of Christ is well known and will outlive all monumental inscription."*  Even more were keen to honour the name of Christ in the name of the Church.  However, members of modern Churches of Christ would not have agreed with some of the practices of John Glas and his son-in-law, Robert Sandeman.  They maintained the Presbyterian practice of infant baptism (sprinkling), rather than adopting the Scriptural principle of adult immersion, "believers' baptism."  Nevertheless, men soon rose up who would quickly and readily embrace the Biblical doctrine of immersion and set it in place in their congregations. Robert Carmichael left the Seceder Presbyterian ministry in 1762 and established an Independent church in Edinburgh. The same year he published a document, 'Declaration and Confession.' In it he stated, *"Christ's kingdom is altogether spiritual. There can be no such thing as a National Church. The Word of God alone is the test of orthodoxy, and there is no Church of Christ other than a society of Christ's disciples called to observe all the ordinances He hath commanded."*

In 1765, Carmichael along with Archibald McLean and five others were immersed into Christ. Congregations based on the teachings of Carmichael and McLean sprang up in many parts of Scotland. At first, they bore the name 'Scotch Baptist.' It was appropriate in that they were Scottish, having no connection with English Baptists and they were Baptists in that they believed, taught and practiced immersion. It was inappropriate in that it was not Biblical. Within two generations, some of these congregations gave up the name 'Scotch Baptist' and took the name 'Churches of Christ.' Churches of Christ today would identify with them. Indeed modern Churches of Christ in Scotland are directly descended from them. The congregation in Kirkcaldy is a good example. It was founded in 1798 as an offshoot of the Scotch Baptist congregation that met in Bristo Place, Edinburgh. The congregation met in the Rose Street chapel. It still meets today at Hayfield Road, Kirkcaldy.

## Review of European Backgrounds

A brief review of our deliberations will help us to keep everything in mind and in place. Reformation roots lie in Wycliffe's England of the 14th century and in Luther and Zwingli's Germany and Switzerland of the 16th century, the same time as the Radical Reformation came about. Its adherents called themselves 'Brethren' but church history knows them as the 'Anabaptists.' From Zurich, the 'Anabaptist' movement progressed down the Rhine through Luther's Germany to Holland. There, in 1536, Menno Simons took up the cause. His followers came to be known as 'Mennonites', a term which slowly replaced 'Anabaptists' among outsiders and has certainly outlasted it. The Mennonite Church is still with us today, mainly in the USA. At first, it seems Anabaptists baptised by affusion (pouring). However, very quickly in accordance with their study of Scripture they moved to immersion and for them that soon became the defining point between the world and the church. In Amsterdam English non-conformists in an Independent congregation met Mennonite teaching early in the 17th century. From there they took the teaching on baptism back to England where congregations calling themselves Churches of Christ arose throughout the 17th century. This teaching came to Scotland with the armies of Cromwell in 1650. There are records of immersion from this time. However, this did not last. The Churches established by these Christian soldiers vanished as quickly as the Commonwealth troops left Scotland in 1659. Nevertheless, a separate though similar process produced Churches of Christ in Scotland in the 18th century. From there the Restoration Movement, as we refer to it after 1800, crossed the Atlantic to America early in the 19th century. At that time, Thomas and Alexander Campbell referred to it as 'the present reformation.' In America, native restoration movements such as that under Barton Stone were in progress and need to be recognised. It would also be interesting to know if any 'Anabaptist' teaching travelled to America in the days of the Pilgrim Fathers and thereafter. To end with a short statement to summarise all of this: Restoration movements proceeded individually and collectively over a period of about 500 years (1380-1850). The battle was long and hard. That is not surprising. The reformers had to overcome 1000 years of apostasy (313-1380). These dates reflect significant events in church history. In 313 Christianity was recognised by the Roman Emperor Constantine in the Edict of Milan. In one way, this was good. In the short term, it ended 250 years of fierce persecution that had begun with Nero in 64 AD. In another way, it was bad in that it tied church and state together and that was responsible for much apostasy over the long term including the development of the Papacy and the medieval Roman Church. After a millennium, the Papacy reached the zenith of its power in the 13th century. It would take another half a millennium to undo the effects of the great apostasy. Arguably, the process was begun by John Wycliffe who died in 1384. Other movements to reform and purify the church predate Wycliffe. These are known by the names, Cathari, Waldensians and the like. However, these were so persecuted that their testimony did not last. Wycliffe and his followers, the Lollards, began a reforming idea that would last. Indeed, we can trace a direct line of reform right back to this time. The process took many twists and turns and involved many people. They built on the accomplishments of preceding generations and we are heirs of that heritage. By 1847 when Alexander Campbell returned on a visit to Britain from America, Churches of Christ were well established.

## Review of British Backgrounds

The Church of England was established by King Henry VIII and advanced by Protestant Reformers in the reign of Queen Elizabeth I. 'Established' meant that it was the

State Church with rights and privileges. It existed by royal assent and enjoyed royal patronage. It benefited from tithing which meant that everyone paid a tenth of their income in taxation, which went to the church. Everyone who was born within the realm was considered a member of this church. You were born into it and the sign of that was baptism, this being the sprinkling of infants. Really, infant 'baptism' accomplished three things in Anglican thinking. It secured forgiveness from the curse of original sin. It signified that the new life was part of the church. It gave a baby a name, which was recorded by the clergyman for civil, and government purposes. The government relied on the church a lot in those days and the church relied on the government. It was a comfortable arrangement. The church supported the government in civil affairs and the government supported the church in religious matters. Of course, not all who were 'baptised' grew up to be conscientious with regard to their faith. The church, in embracing every citizen embraced everything from the pious to the lukewarm to the rogues and villains. To many, this was a less than satisfactory situation. Reform had not gone far enough. They wanted to purify the church. These radicals were given the name 'Puritans.' At first, they stayed within the Episcopal system of ecclesiastical government. Their leaders were Thomas Cartwright (1535-1603) and William Perkins (1558-1602). Elizabeth and her successor James I withstood the Puritans. Later, extreme radicals set up a Separatist movement. Early Separatist leaders were Robert Browne (1550-1633) and Robert Harrison (?-1585). In 1581, they set up a Separatist congregation in Norwich. It was the first Independent or Congregational Church in Britain. They were often called Brownists. At the instigation of the Church of England, the government persecuted them by fines and imprisonment. Many fled to Holland where the Dutch were more tolerant of non-conformists at that time. Brown and Harrison ministered in Middleburg, Zeeland. At one, point Browne visited Scotland. He landed in Dundee in 1584 and travelled via St Andrews to Edinburgh. He lodged in the Canongate and his intent was to establish an Independent congregation as had been done in England and then Holland. The Presbyterian authorities, in the staunch tradition of Knox, opposed him vehemently and drove him out of the city. He returned to England where it is thought he joined the Church of England again.

In Holland Non-conformist activity continued. John Robinson (1576-1625) led one group of Separatists. Later, they made a famous voyage landing at Plymouth Rock, New England in 1620. They are known to history as the Pilgrim Fathers. Another group led by John Smith (1567-1612) and Thomas Helwys (c.1550-1616) met with Mennonites in Amsterdam. There they encountered Anabaptist teaching on baptism. Smith was the first of many to be immersed in 1608. Helwys led the group back to England in 1612. In London, they formed the first Anabaptist congregation at Spittalfields. Church historians call this group General or Arminian Baptists as opposed to the Particular or Calvinistic Baptists who formed another congregation in London in 1638. Both groups came out of that first Independent congregation in Norwich. These early Anabaptist groups were therefore a product of at least two streams, the English Separatists and the Dutch Mennonites. They sought the apostolic pattern for the church, which they believed could be discovered from the New Testament. They believed this was the only legitimate form of church organisation.

By 1660, it is estimated there were 300 Anabaptist congregations in England but the Restoration of the

Monarchy with Charles II in that year brought intolerance and persecution. All Non-conformists were subject to heavy fines and imprisonment. This only ended with the Glorious Revolution of 1688 and the accession of William and Mary. Anabaptists however did not thrive under the new regime of tolerance but due to doctrinal feuds suffered from many self-inflicted wounds. They experienced a new beginning in the second half of the 18th century. At that time, the English Baptists developed their church polity. In 1792 the Baptist Missionary Society was founded and in 1832 the Baptist Union. This marked the start of the modern Baptist movement. In Scotland, beginning in 1765, the Scotch Baptists developed independently of the English Baptist order and their movement would feed into the Restoration Movement.

# PART TWO

–

# SCOTLAND: REFORMATION TO RESTORATION

# CHAPTER 3

# PRESBYTERIANISM

At the beginning of the sixteenth century, Scotland stood in great need of national reformation. An inept monarchy, a feuding aristocracy and a corrupt clergy had maintained Scotland's place as a backwater of Renaissance Europe. For over a thousand years before that, indeed back to Roman times, it had been no better. However, Scotland was to be radically changed. Within three hundred years, Scotland had made such advances in education, invention and innovation that, it took a leading place in Europe and the world. What led to such a transformation? The Reformation!

The beginnings of the Reformation are to be found in the mountain heartland of Europe. There, men such as John Huss, Martin Luther and John Calvin in trying to reform their own Roman Catholic Church were actually to break the mould of a thousand years. It also shaped the thinking of Haddington's most famous son, John Knox. He had to flee Scotland for Geneva. He finally returned to Scotland from Europe in 1559. He brought Reformation principles. On prior occasions, he had not been successful. This time however he succeeded. By 1560, the first Book of Discipline and the Scots Confession had been published. From there the Church of Scotland, Presbyterian in nature, was established as the religion of the nation. In England, Episcopacy had been established with the monarch as the head of the Church of England. This tied church and state almost absolutely, the monarch ruling through the bishops. In Scotland, throughout most of the seventeenth century, there was a hard and bitter conflict to resist such a system. These were the days of the Covenanters. The leaders were men such as Richard Cameron, from whom the Cameronian regiment took its name, Donald Cargill and James Renwick, the last martyr to be hanged in the year 1688. However, even in Scotland the ties between church and state were very strong. In the beginning, this may well have been necessary to stand against the power of Rome. Presbyterianism in Scotland was quickly consolidated by Knox and other able men. Let no one think that what was accomplished in Scotland was done by Knox alone. For a century, the Reformation absorbed the best of the nation's resources and produced a succession of men who ably supported the Protestant cause. Among them were scholars, teachers, preachers, writers and administrators. There was Melville, Welsh, Craig, Pollock, Davidson, Bruce, Calderwood, Boyd, Cameron, Henderson, Rutherford, Gillespie, Baillie, Dickson, Hutcheson, Ferguson, Blair, Wood, Gray, Binning, Guthrie, Livingstone, Durham, Carstares, Rule, Forrester, Jameson, Lauder, Park, Anderson, Woodrow, Monro, Shields, Renwick, Halyburton, Cunningham and Boston. From such a list the sheer manpower, the ability and vitality which went into the Reformation can be appreciated. Protestant theology now ruled Scotland as absolutely and ironically, as intolerantly as had Roman Catholic theology. For a century, the reformed faith remained unchallenged and dominated Scotland. Presbyterianism had a secure foundation. However, a book appeared and an issue arose that was to change the course of Presbyterian Church history.

The book was 'The Marrow of Modern Divinity' published in 1726 by Thomas Boston of Ettrick. Boston himself had been impressed by an earlier work by Kemperis, 'The Image of Christ.' The book had a profound effect on Protestant theology. Boston's stand left traditional Calvinism for a more Arminian and evangelical viewpoint. Many were so influenced, among them Henry Davidson of Galashiels and Gabriel Wilson of Maxton. It was not until 1733, nearly two hundred years after the Reformation, that any divergence was found within Presbyterianism. At that time, Ebenezer and Ralph Erskine founded the Secession Church. It came about in this way. In 1712, the right of the people to choose their own minister was removed by the new Union Parliament of 1707. (The Union of the Crowns of Scotland and England had taken place in 1603 when James VI of Scotland became James I of Great Britain.) Patronage was restored, but for twenty years, patrons and presbyteries were careful to appoint ministers acceptable to the people. Then in 1731 the General Assembly, the ruling body of the Church of Scotland, adopted parliament's view. Now the appointment of ministers in the view of the government and the church rested with patrons, usually the powerful landowning families. The Erskines along with three other ministers opposed this act so vehemently that they were expelled from the General Assembly in 1732. Beginning in 1733 with four congregations and less than one thousand members, the Secession Church increased to one hundred and twenty congregations and one hundred thousand members by 1765. Of course, this was mostly a result of people leaving the established church. In 1747, a division occurred within the Seceders as to whether church members could swear to part of the oath taken by Burgesses, officials of certain Scottish towns known as burghs. This led to the formation of the General Associate Synod (Anti-burgers) and the Associate Synod (Burgers) in 1749.

In 1751 Thomas Gillespie, minister of Carnock Parish near Dunfermline, was deposed by the General Assembly of the Church of Scotland for refusing to assist in the induction of a new minister in the parish of Inverkeithing. The candidate had been presented by his patron but refused by the people. The people supported Gillespie though he had to preach in the fields. Much the same happened in Jedburgh and Colinsburgh. The men chosen by the people were Thomas Boston Jr. and Thomas Collier. Together, with Gillespie, they formed the Presbytery of Relief in 1761 or as it is better known, the Relief Church. The 'relief' referred to being relief from patronage. Before the close of the eighteenth century, many in both Seceder Synods began to place a lesser importance on the connection between church and state. This was a new approach but those holding it stated that people should be amenable to 'new light' from Scripture, hence, the division in both Synods between 'Auld Lichts' and 'New Lichts.' During this time, within the mainstream Presbyterianism of 'the Kirk', a sharp division arose between the so-called 'Moderates' and 'Evangelicals.' Thomas Boston had triggered the debate. Men such as William Robertson (Moderate) and John Witherspoon (Evangelical) carried it on through the second half of the eighteenth century. The period also saw the effects of the English 'Great Awakening' in Scotland. George Whitfield's first visit to Scotland in 1742 and the mighty 'Revivals' at Cambuslang and Kilsyth had a profound effect on men such as John Erskine, minister at Kirkintilloch. He corresponded with the English evangelist, John Newton, commending him but stating his surprise that Newton could stay in a church that taught baptismal regeneration. Newton replied that he was surprised that Erskine could stay in a church that tolerated Dr. Robertson of the Moderate faction! An example of the conflict is seen in the 1796 General Assembly where the Reverend Hamilton of Gladsmuir, a Moderate, advocated that people should be educated and civilised first so that the Gospel could follow. Erskine replied 'Moderator rax me (hand me) that Bible.' He proceeded to read Luke's account of Paul on the island of Malta, pointing out that the apostle did not wait to first educate and civilise the people before preaching the Gospel. The Evangelicals were firm in their commitment to 'the Gospel first.' This was one of the factors which led to the formation of the Free Church of Scotland in 1843, led by the renowned Evangelical, Thomas Chalmers. In 1847, the Relief Church and the United Secession Church merged to form the United Presbyterian Church. In 1900, the Free Church and the United Presbyterian Church merged to form the United Free Church of Scotland. A minority of Free Church congregations maintained their own identity to become popularly known as 'the Wee Frees.' In 1916, the theological schools of the Church of Scotland and the United Free Church merged. The sixteenth century Reformation established a successful break from oppressive Romanism where prior attempts had failed. The first Reformers laid a foundation upon which others would build. Within Presbyterianism, the eighteenth century rise of the Secession and Relief Churches showed that change was possible. A far more tolerant attitude was seen than had existed in previous centuries. The evangelistic nature of the Free Church demonstrated men's fervour for the Gospel. We have seen some of the main progressive movements within the Reformed faith. However the Presbyterian system, a great land mark though it was, had its own self-imposed limitations. Now we must go out-with 'the established church' to the so-called 'non-conformist faiths' to follow the struggle for truth.

# CHAPTER 4

# NON-CONFORMISM

Somebody said, "How profitable the Scriptures must be for men to study them so." In the sixteenth and seventeenth centuries, scholars were translating the Bible into the languages of the people. From the fifth century, the Latin Vulgate version of Jerome had been the only translation available. To the vast majority of people the Bible was a closed book. They could not read Latin and thought it no more than a book of ecclesiastical formulas which supported the rituals of the medieval Roman church. Now, new translations of the Bible in the language of the people were turning the Scriptures into a mighty power. For this, we must acknowledge with gratitude the contributions of men such as John Wycliffe, William Tyndale, Myles Coverdale and others. From academics in the great seats of learning, to the ordinary man and woman, people were interested in the Bible. They were not interested in supporting an ecclesiastical system or fulfilling religious rituals, but rather in seeing what the Bible said on a whole host of subjects. Conforming to the Bible admonition of 'being not hearers only but doers,' they were soon applying its truths.

Who knows why it is that one subject has always thrown up a sharp divide between those who 'hear and do' and those who 'hear but do not do?' That subject is the subject of baptism. In the seventeenth century, many concluded that conversion was necessary and that it was necessarily an adult concern. They saw a clear Scriptural truth, namely that penitent believers must be baptised in order to enter the kingdom of God. They were called 'Anabaptists' meaning 'baptised again.' They would never have held with this since they did not recognise infant baptism. In Europe, Balthasar Hubmaier had put this view forward in the sixteenth century. Anabaptist teaching spread to Holland where the Mennonite Church originated based on the work of Menno Simons. They were later known by the name 'Brethren.' As early as the end of the sixteenth century some English refugees in Amsterdam had encountered such teaching. One who was influenced by it was John Smith who became a pioneer of Anabaptist views in England in the seventeenth century. There his views were to take root. Scotland also saw some non-conformist activity. Robert Browne had been driven to Flanders because of Episcopalian persecution in England. Then with several companions and families, he came to Scotland, landing at Dundee at the close of 1583. He then travelled to Edinburgh where he took up residence at the head of the Canongate on the 9th of January 1584. However, the Church of Scotland opposed his congregational views just as the Church of England had done. On the 21st of January, the local Presbytery examined him. By the 17th of July, he had returned to England having accomplished little. Nevertheless, the Anabaptist cause continued in other places. John Penry was one of the first martyrs for Independency. In 1624, Congregationalism, called Brownism at that time, re-appeared in Scotland. The main influence was Henry Jacob of London. The movement was very much an underground one. Calderwood, writing in his 'History of the Kirk of Scotland' commented, "such seeds of separation have brought forth damned sects of Anabaptists, Families of Love, Brownists...and manie such pests." Hardly surprising, since Knox himself opposed all non-conformist sentiments calling them "maist horribill and absurd." Gilbert Gardin of Tulliefruskie was excommunicated for his Anabaptist views. In 1647, Robert Baillie published a book on Anabaptists in the hope of preventing the spread of 'this pest' to Scotland. No longer however was the religious situation a simple divide between 'Papist' and 'Protestant.' Nicholl's diary for 1651 records the names "Covenanter, Anti-covenanter, Puritan, Roundhead, Separatist, Malignant, Sectary, Quaker and Anabaptist." Anabaptist religion came to Scotland in a curious way. Robert Brown's non-conformism had been successfully resisted in 1584 by the Presbyterian establishment with the approval and sanction of the Crown. However in 1650 the power of the Crown itself was swept away with the coming of the Commonwealth. The Puritanism of Oliver Cromwell was far more tolerant of the Anabaptists than had been the old regime of the Crown and the established churches of England and Scotland. Indeed, many of Cromwell's own men were Anabaptists so a ready-made missionary force went wherever the Commonwealth army went. In Scotland, there were eighteen garrison towns and four citadels, Perth, Leith, Ayr and Inverness. Anabaptist congregations were established by Cromwellian soldiers. The best example is Leith. The citadel there was governed by Major-General Lillburne, commander of the army in Scotland and an Anabaptist. A congregation was established in 1652 and a pamphlet of 1653 said the church met every Sunday, alternating between Leith and the Tolbooth in Edinburgh. Nicholl, the diarist, records immersions taking place through the week, writing "some dippit at Bonnington Mill, betwixt Leith and Edinburgh, both men and women of good rank." Thus, many of the local inhabitants came into the congregation as well as many soldiers.    The Leith congregation had close ties with Anabaptist congregations in England, particularly Hexham and Fenstanton.  In 1652 Edward Hickhorngill, a preacher, was sent by the church in Hexham to minister to the church in Leith.    Later, he resigned and he was succeeded by Thomas Stackhouse.    Incidentally, Hickhorngill later confessing to be an atheist was disfellowshipped by the Leith congregation.  This was recognised by Hexham who sent a letter of admonition after which Hickhorngill was restored.  The Perth congregation was referred to in a letter of Hickhorngill to Hexham in 1653.    There General Overton was governor and again an Anabaptist.   George Fox, the Quaker, called them "rude janglers and disputers." At Ayr, where the remains of the citadel were evident until very recently, a Captain Spence had gathered twenty-three corporals and privates into an Anabaptist society.   In Fife, the diarist Lamont recorded that in 1652 at Cupar, where Colonel Fairfax's regiment was based, Chaplain Brown preached the Gospel and baptised several soldiers in the River Eden.  The records of the Church of Scotland at Cupar noted that in 1658 "Christina Myllar was excommunicated for persisting in Anabaptism and other errors."  In Aberdeen, there was much Anabaptist activity. Bishop Burnet in his 'History,' a record of his own time, remembers as a boy the coming of three Cromwellian regiments, most being Independents and Anabaptists. Their preacher was Samuel Oattes.  He had a great influence. Church of Scotland ministers, John Forbes of Kincardine and William Youngson of Durris both declared themselves Anabaptists.  Similar events were happening throughout

Scotland. Alex Cornwall, parish minister at Linlithgow, was immersing people and came under sentence of excommunication by the Church of Scotland. One of the leading Anabaptists in Scotland was Lady Craigie-Wallace who maintained her Anabaptist testimony to her death in 1663. Thomas Charteris of Stonehouse maintained Anabaptist doctrine and would not baptise infants. Charteris had moved from Edinburgh, 'having been appointed to the rich living of Kilbride Parish' where he formed a congregation of thirty. The church at Hexham also sent Edward Limburgh to minister at Jedburgh. A letter was written by one William Packer to encourage Anabaptist soldiers at Holmdell (Helmsdale) in Sutherland. A reply was written by one Jonas Dell, "In opposition to those dipping themselves in water." Anabaptists utilised the new printing process. Two pamphlets were published by the Leith church. The first was 'The Baptist Confession of Faith' of 1644 and the second, 'Heart Bleedings for Professor's Abominations' of 1653. The title page disclaimed the name 'Anabaptist' and stated its aim as 'the vindication of the truth and information of the ignorant.' All this was remarkable progress in fair weather indeed. However, storms were to follow. The appointment of Oliver Cromwell as Lord Protector caused a serious division within Scots Anabaptists. Those with republican views opposed Cromwell. The rest supported him. Many Anabaptist officers were accused of sedition including General Overton, Majors Holmes, Harrison and Branston, Captain Hedworth and Chaplain Oattes. In 1655, they appealed to Cromwell for vindication and published, 'The Humble Address of the Baptised Churches consisting of officers, soldiers and others walking in Gospel order at Leith, Edinburgh and St Johnstone.' Those opposed replied in 'Reasons against communion with those who signed the Address.' The strife within the Commonwealth army led to the suppression of the whole Anabaptist movement. In 1658, Cromwell ordered that no Anabaptist hold any office of trust, practice at law or keep a school. General Monk, having no Anabaptist sympathies, willingly complied. Presbyterians were now favoured over all Anabaptists. Anabaptists in public positions were dismissed. Officers were imprisoned in Tantallon Castle. This severe purge weakened the Anabaptist cause but they hung on. An appeal for toleration in July 1659 was unsuccessful. In November 1659, the Commonwealth army left Edinburgh as suddenly as it had arrived. Anabaptist congregations throughout Scotland were depleted as all soldier-members left. In 1660, the monarchy was restored under Charles II. Active Anabaptist life in Scotland disappeared under stern measures, far more severe than anything that had gone before. On the 2nd of January 1661, a Royal Proclamation was read at the Mercat Crosses of Royal Burghs. It was against Quakers and Anabaptists 'to apprehend any such persons as shall frequent such meetings.' An act of 1662 stated that parents of any child un-baptised after thirty days were subject to heavy fines. The act was applied vigorously as Sheriffs were allowed to keep these fines. The result was that many Anabaptists left the country and others renounced their beliefs. Those who remained were unable to meet or teach publicly.

Thus, the Anabaptist movement of the seventeenth century was short but it was important. It was a period of enlightenment. One commentator said, "The English were more indulgent to the Scots than the Scots were to themselves." Truly, Cromwell's troops were not only interested in the religious life of the people but in education, justice and civil improvement. More importantly, more people had responded to a religious plea than in any period since the Reformation itself.  By the Restoration of the monarchy in 1660, every village had a school, almost every family had a Bible and most children could read them.  The flower had bloomed and withered but the seeds had been sown and they would bear fruit in a later age.

# CHAPTER 5

# INDEPENDENCY

The eighteenth century saw a great many developments in the religious climate of Scotland. Remember that within Presbyterianism, the Secession Church had been established in 1733, the Relief Church in 1761 and the Moderate-Evangelical controversy was in full flood. These movements although breaking with the established church, the Church of Scotland, did remain within the Presbyterian fold. Other movements originating in Presbyterianism were to develop out-with the Reformed faith while others were descended from the Anabaptist movement of the previous century. It is to these independent movements that we now turn our attention.

## The Glasites

John Glas is widely regarded as 'the father of Scottish Congregationalism.' He was born on the 21st of September 1695 at Auchtermuchty in Fife. His father, Alexander, was a minister of the Kirk. When John was five years old, the family moved to Kinclaven. He was educated at Perth Grammar School and St Andrews University where he graduated from St Leonards College in 1713. He was ordained and inducted into Tealing Parish, five miles north of Dundee, in 1719. He married Catherine Black, a minister's daughter, and set about ministering to a parish of around 750 people. His powerful preaching attracted large crowds. He supported Presbyterianism and the National Covenant but the over-zealous nature of some of his parishioners for the Covenant made him think. Conversation with two colleagues, Willison and Archibald, set him to study the nature of the relationship between church and state. Ebenezer Erskine, later to establish the Secession Church, read one of Glas's papers and wrote expressing appreciation of his study. Glas stated with regard to the National Covenant, "I am resolved, if possible, to be at the bottom of this controversy and that it should be determined to me by the word of the Lord Jesus and by that only." Glas never thought that taking the Word of God as his sole rule of conduct would bring him into collision with his church but it did. His conclusions were devastating. After his study, he stated, "National Christianity is not New Testament Christianity. There is no New Testament authority for the National Covenant or the Solemn League and Covenant. Magistrates have no function in Christ's Church. They cannot punish heresy. Political and secular weapons rather than Christ's Word and Spirit are wrong in the church." Glas then had the courage to preach that in which he believed. Throughout the summer of 1726 at Fowlis, Longforgan and other places Glas preached, "apart from the New Testament in Christ's blood there was no other covenant in the New Testament Church." Strong feelings were aroused, some refusing communion if Glas was present. Willison warned that if Glas persisted with his views he would oppose him publicly. Glas refused to be silent, inviting Willison's response in light of the serious nature of the question. On the 6th of August 1726, Glas and Willison were to preach at the Strathmartine communion. Glas asked William Thomson, minister at Strathmartine to find a substitute for him but no one was forthcoming. Glas preached on John 6:69, the threefold office of Christ as prophet, priest and king. He pointed out from John 18:36-37 that "Christ testified plainly that His Kingdom is not a worldly kingdom and that it is not set up, advanced or defended as the kingdoms of this world." Willison defended the National Covenant, "the glory of Scotland" and said that opposition to it was opposition to the national confession of faith and the national church. Glas was ostracised by ministers of adjoining parishes. He was called to account before the Dundee presbytery on the 6th of September 1726. At the October presbytery meeting, he was asked to keep silence on the dispute but he refused, saying that he could not compromise the truth. The synod meeting at Montrose on the 17th of October 1727 set up a committee to investigate the whole matter. It did so and put questions to Glas on twenty-six matters at the Brechin Synod of April 1728. The final decision was to censure Glas and suspend him pending repentance. Glas appealed to the General Assembly and he was heard on the 11th of May that year. He was supported by elders, deacons and members from Tealing. On the 18th of May, he appeared before the assembly with two elders, David Gray and Thomas Wallace. The commission appointed to deal with the matter backed the Brechin Synod's decision. Glas continued to preach in Tealing. The case continued through July, August and September. Finally, on the 15th of October 1728, in accordance with the Acts of Assembly of 1648 Glas was deposed as a minister of the Church of Scotland. He again appealed but his appeal was not heard until the General Assembly of May 1729. In March 1730, Glas again appeared before a select commission. He was supported by ministers Thomas Boston of Ettrick, Henry

Davidson of Galashiels, Gabriel Wilson of Maxton and Moderator Hamilton. James Hog, Ebenezer and Ralph Erskine were in favour of severe measures. None had at any time tried to show Glas's views to be in error. Nevertheless, the commission supported the deposition by a narrow margin. The deposition of John Glas was the first instance of such action in the Church of Scotland. Later, in 1739, Glas was given another opportunity to repent by the General Assembly who, even then, recognised him as a minister of the Gospel but not of the established church. However, by then it was too late. Glas continued to preach and although many former parishioners fell away, some remained with him. He moved into Dundee and there, in the home of Baillie George Lyon, formed a small congregation, the first Glasite church. But how would it be organised? His own father was the first to tell him that he was really a Congregationalist. His father-in-law told him that what he aimed for never could nor would take place. Glas's conviction was this, "the Scriptures of the Old and New Testament contain the complete revelation of the whole counsel of God and are the perfect rule of the Christian religion which is still to be found pure and entire in these." He studied the rise of the Roman hierarchy from the simple ministry of the New Testament. He made a distinction between extra-ordinary officers (apostles and prophets) and ordinary officers (elders and deacons). He agreed with Presbyterians that the office of bishop and elder were one and the same. He insisted on a plurality of elders in each congregation. No clergy-laity distinctions were made. Ecclesiastical titles were shunned. Elders would normally work in everyday occupations but if required, support from the church would be quite proper. He maintained that it was quality of character that was important in elders and not a university education, as was commonly held at the time. The organisation of the church based on the authority of the Bible was important to Glas. As he put it, "This ministry is God's gift to His church, invested with divine authority, possessing functions which may not be assumed by any except those specially chosen and ordained to office. Without a complete presbytery no church is complete or may observe the institutions and discipline appointed by Christ" Another area of great importance was the Lord's Supper. He believed it was intended that each congregation of the body of Christ should partake and that this communion should be weekly. He rejected any idea of transubstantiation, saying of the feast, "while it is a real communion of the body and blood of Christ, the sign must not be confused with that which is signified, viz. the sacrificial death of Christ. That sacrifice has been made once for all and cannot be repeated in the sacrament which represents it and assures its benefits." With regard to creeds and confessions of faith, Glas admitted that in opposing error it might be useful for a church to publish its faith and interpretation of the Word of God. However, he denied these any authoritative value. On the subject of baptism, his views remained unchanged from his Presbyterian days, saying that the blood of Christ saved sinners and that baptism by sprinkling should be administered to believers and their children. Glas placed a strong emphasis on fellowship, believing in mutual exhortation and helping needy members through the use of regular contributions. Other practises included the use of love feasts, the holy kiss, foot-washing and strict discipline.

The first Glasite congregation came into being on the 13th of July 1725 with nearly one hundred members on the roll. This first group in Tealing remained within the bounds of the Church of Scotland but met in small 'societies' for prayer and exhortation. It was when Glas moved to Dundee after his deposition from the established church that the first independent Glasite church was formed. A minister from Guthrie, Francis Archibald, joined Glas in the eldership. Glas was initially supported by friends and then by setting up a bookshop. Two more elders were appointed. James Cargill remained at Dundee with Glas. William Scott became a co-pastor of Archibald at Guthrie. In 1733, a congregation was formed at Perth under the eldership of James Don and James Cant who remained in office for forty years. In 1734, a congregation was formed in Edinburgh and there a sixteen-year-old student, Robert Sandeman, joined the movement. His father, David, had business connections with the congregation in Dundee. Sandeman was to have a great influence on the movement. He married Glas's eldest daughter, Catherine, and in 1744 he was ordained as an elder at Perth. Meanwhile in 1738 another young man had come into the movement. He was George Byers who had succeeded his father as minister of the Church of Scotland at Lessuden, St Boswells, in 1730. Incidentally, Byers married a daughter of Gabriel Wilson, minister at Maxton. Sandeman and Byers later served as elders in Edinburgh. Through Sandeman's preaching and writing, the views of the Glasite movement spread as far as England, Wales and New England in what would become the United States of America. Indeed Sandeman visited New England and he died and was buried at Danbury, Connecticut.

In 1757, Robert Carmichael, minister of the Anti-burger Secession church at Coupar Angus, became associated with the Glasite movement. He was dissatisfied with the Secession church and his case before the synod ended with his deposition in 1763. Carmichael along with Archibald

Mclean, a Glasgow bookseller, became active in the Glasite church in Glasgow. However, in 1763 Carmichael and McLean withdrew from the Glasite movement over the issue of church discipline. Also in 1763, John Glas moved to Edinburgh and then, in 1764, to Glasgow where he was joined by James Don, an elder from Arbroath. In 1769, Glas retired to Dundee. During this time, the movement was joined by another two men who, like Carmichael and McLean, were to have a great influence on Scottish church history. They were both ministers in the Church of Scotland. One was Robert Ferrier of Largo and the other, James Smith of the adjoining parish of Newburn in Fife. John Glas died on the 2nd of November 1773 in his seventy-eighth year, the fifty-fifth of his ministry. He was buried in 'The Old Howff' cemetery in Dundee. His monument reads, "John Glas, Minister of the Congregational Church in this place, died November 1773 aged 78 years. His Character in the Churches of Christ is well known and will outlive all monumental inscriptions." His wife, Catherine, had died in 1749. Of their fifteen children, Thomas became an elder in Dundee. There can be no doubt that Glas's influence was tremendous. Certainly, it was out of all proportion to the size or the number of congregations established. In Scotland Congregational churches after the order of John Glas existed in Aberdeen, Arbroath, Cupar, Dundee, Dunkeld, Edinburgh, Galashiels, Glasgow, Guthrie, Leith, Leslie, Paisley and Perth. Glas was a diligent Bible student, proficient in Hebrew and Greek and well acquainted with the works of the great religious writers down through the centuries. His own literary output was enormous. His 'Notes on Scripture Texts,' written from 1747 to 1760, extended to seven volumes. His greatest work was 'The Testimony of the King of Martyrs.' He placed little emphasis on academic learning as a qualification for Christian ministry yet had a thorough education himself. He was a man of independent judgment and critical ability. He subjected every theory and practice to the touchstone of Scripture. He was a good preacher and he gave his last sermon a week before his death. Contemporaries relate that he was warmhearted, he loved children and he had a genius for making friends. In 1760 one visitor from London recalled, "He was the most truly reverent and yet ardent bishop I know of in Christendom at present. Profound, indefatigable, studious, yet cheerful and always gay. How easy his learning and religion sit upon him." His friends knew him as 'Jock.'

Outside of Scotland, Glasite churches were formed in London (1761), Wooler, Newcastle, Gayle, Newby, Kirkby Stephen, Kirkby Lonsdale, Whitehaven, Kendal, Colne, Liverpool, York, Nottingham, Trowbridge (Wiltshire), Old Buckenham (Norfolk), Weathersfield (Essex), Swansea (1766), Carmarthen, Llangadock and Llangyfelach. Robert Sandeman, through his tours and writings, had a great influence in the spread of Glas's ideas. Along with William Sandeman and John Handasyde of Wooler, he visited London in 1761 to establish that congregation. They were assisted by John Barnard, an Independent minister in Islington. Sandeman had contacted Barnard and two colleagues, William Cudworth and Samuel Pike through his 'Letters on Theron and Aspasio.' The correspondence also attracted the attention of William Jones in 'The New Evangelical Magazine.' The movement also gained from close ties with the societies formed by Benjamin Ingham in England.

### Sir William Sinclair and the Church at Keiss

Sir William Sinclair was in military service at Portsmouth when he first encountered the Anabaptist movement and he was immersed. His father, Sir James, created a baronet in 1704, but an immoral man, died in 1742. Sir William then took over the family estate at Keiss in Caithness. He himself preached the Gospel and a church was formed on New Year's Day, 1750. It met in the ruins of the old castle. A visitor in 1762, Robert Forbes, found them practising such things as baptism, weekly communion, love feasts and foot washing. The congregation numbered about thirty. In 1763, Sinclair went to Edinburgh on pressing financial business. He left the congregation in the care of John Budge, his land steward, whom he had immersed into Christ. Budge was described by the local parish minister as "a zealous Anabaptist." In Edinburgh Sinclair made contact with John Glas and Robert Sandeman. He worshipped with them for a while but doctrinal differences prevented any union. There is no record that he ever encountered the Scotch Baptist congregation established in 1765. Sinclair died in 1768. With regard to the Church at Keiss, little is known after 1763. John Budge visited Edinburgh in 1790. At that time, he concluded that the church should not celebrate the Lord's Supper without an elder being present. James Haldane noted this on his first tour, preaching at nearby Freswick in October 1797. Budge died in 1800 and he was succeeded by Donald Inrigg until his death in 1831. His successors were Andrew Rugg and Alexander Bain. The congregation was also aided by Edward Mackay of the Scotch Baptist Church at Thurso. In 1836, membership was about twenty but attendances ranged from thirty to sixty. Mackay visited four to six times a year at which time the Lord's Supper was observed. Robert Sowerby continued this work after Mackay's death in 1845. In 1860, James Scott became pastor. The church was still going in 1880 but thereafter slowly died out. However, the whole venture is interesting in that it shows that churches after the apostolic order can be established without regard to time or place if people are willing to return to the New Testament.

## The Scotch Baptists

We have already seen the influence of the Anabaptist movement in Scotland during the seventeenth century but from the close of the Commonwealth in 1660, it was over a century before similar stirrings would occur. One incident however shows that Anabaptist ideas were not dead, merely dormant. In the early eighteenth century Thomas Lawrie, a Presbyterian minister, was baptised at the Spittalfields church in London. This came to the attention of Baptist ministers in the city. On hearing him preach, they approved his Gospel knowledge but due to his 'Scotch pronunciation' did not recommend him for engagement in the South. Instead, they believed he should return to Scotland where, according to Lawrie, other ministers shared his conviction on baptism. As it turned out Lawrie did not return to Scotland due to illness. A later record of the Closeburn church says he was deposed from the ministry for alleged immorality. After this, the rise of the Scotch Baptists occurred in the mid-eighteenth century. The movement was entirely indigenous. In terms of evangelical doctrine, it shared much in common with the English Baptist movement. In terms of church government, it was very different. These peculiarities won it the name 'Scotch Baptist' in contrast to churches founded upon the English order.

In 1762, Robert Carmichael left his post as a minister of the Anti-burger Secession Church at Coupar Angus. He became a pastor of the Glasite Church in Glasgow. He shared Glas's views concerning the kingdom and church government. In 1763, he met Archibald McLean, a printer and bookseller in Glasgow. He had come to the Glasites from the Church of Scotland. Within a year, both left the Glasites due to a grievance over church discipline that, in their opinion, was too strict. Carmichael moved to Edinburgh to minister to an Independent church. Both were keen Bible students and before they parted, they agreed to a study together. The subject was baptism. In June 1764, Carmichael wrote to McLean for his conclusion. McLean replied saying that the ordinance was reserved for believers and that the mode was immersion. His judgement, he said, was based on his own study of the Bible. Carmichael remained unconvinced and continued in his former thinking, 'baptising' the newborn child of a colleague. Due to doctrinal differences, he withdrew from the Independent church in May 1765. Seven others did the same, one of their number being Dr. Robert Walker. They met in Magdalene Chapel in the Cowgate, Edinburgh, renting it from the Incorporation of Hammermen for £8. Carmichael then came to accept the Scriptural view of baptism advanced by McLean. Five others did the same. They had no knowledge of other Baptist groups or of Sir William Sinclair who was also in Edinburgh at this time. The group asked Dr. Gill of London to come to Edinburgh and baptise them. He referred them to David Ferrie ministering in Durham. He, like Gill, did not come. A second appeal to Dr. Gill brought Carmichael an invitation to London. He went and preached at Dr. Gill's congregation, a Baptist church in the Barbican. It was there Carmichael was baptised on the 9th of October 1765. He then returned to Edinburgh and baptised his five friends. The baptisms took place in the Water of Leith at Canonmills on the 25th of November. The church continued to meet in Magdalene Chapel. Several weeks later Archibald McLean was baptised and moved to Edinburgh, working as a corrector for Donaldson the printer. In

June 1768, McLean was chosen to work with Carmichael in the ministry. Baptists from Hexham and Newcastle, David Ferrie and William Angus, came to encourage the young congregation. People came from Glasgow, Dundee, Montrose and other places to be baptised. A congregation was organised in Dundee and Carmichael moved there in May 1769. Dr. Walker took up the ministry in Edinburgh with McLean. Carmichael was recalled to Edinburgh due to failing health and there he died in March 1774. In 1769, a congregation was established in Glasgow with several being baptised in the River Clyde near the Herd's House at Glasgow Green. McLean moved back to Glasgow and the church met in the High Street from March 1770. Later George Begg was added to the eldership. The Glasite church in Montrose embraced Anabaptist views and in the autumn of 1770 McLean immersed seven men and two women in the River Esk. Elders were appointed, John Greig, David Mill and Thomas Wren. The church had a considerable influence until it faded out in 1855. In the years 1777 to 1780 William Braidwood, Independent minister, Charles Stuart, Church of Scotland minister at Cramond and George Grieve, Presbyterian minister at Wooler joined the movement. Churches were established at Dunfermline and Wooler (1779), Galashiels and Newburgh (1782), Perth (1784) and Largo (1791). The latter was established by Sir John Goodsir, a distinguished surgeon who had been baptised in 1778. Sometime between 1784 and 1786 a congregation was established in Kirkcaldy and in 1798 it was set in order under the eldership of William Peddie and H. Cameron. In 1795, a congregation was established in Paisley by Thomas Watson and William Marshall. In 1792, a congregation had been established in London and by 1795, congregations existed in Chester, Beverly, Hall and Whitehaven. The Liverpool congregation came into being in

1800 under the direction of William Jones and D.S. Wylie. Jones had been baptised by Archibald McLean at Chester in 1786. The Scotch Baptists did not view formal academic training as essential to the ministry although many of their preachers were well trained, most having a Secession Church background. Some of the men involved were James Watt of Glasgow, William Peddie of Edinburgh, Charles Arthur of Kirkcaldy, D.S. Wylie of Paisley, Christopher Anderson and A. Wemyss. Some were associated with the Haldanes as colleagues (William Stephens and Archibald Smith) or as students (Andrew Fuller, George Barclay of Irvine, Edward Mackay of Thurso and John Young of Paisley who subsequently baptised James Haldane).

In the years 1800 to 1820, congregations were established at the rate of two every year. The evangelical tour of James Watt in 1797 led to churches being established at New Pitsligo (1803), Aberchirder (1808), St Fergus (1809) and Fraserburgh (1810) as well as Scotch Baptist families at Balmand, Portsoy, Banff, Inchture and other places. However, the movement had many problems. Division resulted from doctrinal issues (for example, the nature of the Godhead) and practical matters (for example, how many members constitute a church?) Division was seen in Edinburgh, Glasgow, Dundee, Paisley, Dunfermline, Aberdeen and Liverpool. One good point was that each local congregation was autonomous and so it could control its own destiny rather than being swept away by wholesale apostasy. The doctrine of these Scotch Baptist churches was summarised in Rippon's register of 1795 as follows: "no human traditions were admitted, the New Testament being very plain on matters of faith and practice. The church was strictly congregational with unanimity being required on decisions. Discipline was strict and impartial to maintain purity. They continued in the Apostles' doctrine and met every first day of the week for the observance of Scripture reading and preaching, fellowship or contribution, the Lord's Supper, prayer and singing. Some congregations optionally practised the love feast for the poor, the kiss of charity and foot washing. Christians were to submit to civil power in all lawful matters. They were to dress modestly and abstain from eating blood. Marriage was permitted only in the Lord."

What happened to these Scotch Baptists? George Yuille in his 'History of Baptists in Scotland' says, "Scotch Baptist Churches in England numbered at least twenty, apart from a dozen in the Welsh group of which J.R. Jones of Ramoth was the leader. Most of these became Baptist, three or four survived in Lancashire, some joined the Churches of Christ. Some Scotch Baptist Churches in Scotland also joined the Churches of Christ before 1840 as at Auchtermuchty, Dumfries, Newmilns and Stevenston."

Significantly, Scotch Baptist groups, like Haldanite groups, crossed the Atlantic and congregations were established in a few of the cities of the eastern seaboard like Boston, New York and Philadelphia. The significance of this lies in the fact that Scotch Baptist ideas then fed into the Restoration Movement in the United States. Although Scotch Baptist churches died out in the U.S. as they did back home in Scotland and England, principles they stood for and ideas they put forward advanced into new congregations that came forth. The Restoration Movement benefited from this.

William Jones, who was baptised by Archibald McLean in 1786, established the Scotch Baptist Church in Liverpool in 1800. By 1835 Jones was an elder in the Scotch Baptist

Church in Windmill Street, Finsbury Square, London. He published Alexander Campbell's Millennial Harbinger in Britain. He contacted Campbell of the Restoration Movement in the USA through a young American art student, Peyton C. Wyeth of Pennsylvania who was visiting London. James Wallis, a clothier, was a Scotch Baptist in Nottingham. He did not entirely agree with their doctrine however and on the 25th December 1836, he and thirteen others withdrew to form a congregation after the New Testament pattern. By the end of 1837, there were ninety-seven members and Wallis was publishing the influential 'Christian Messenger' and later 'the British Millennial Harbinger.'

Like the churches of John Glas, the Scotch Baptists for all their shortcomings did arise with an eager desire to attain a purer and more ardent life than seemed possible in the established churches of that day. It is to their credit that they earnestly searched the New Testament for the primitive church order, believing that this was nearest to the mind of Christ and so alone was legitimate. Unfortunately, they came to exalt the letter above the spirit. The order and constitution of the church thus came to be considered of supreme importance above all else. It is not by a spirit of legalism that churches live but by their possession of the spirit of Christ. The lack of evangelical character finally caused the decline and extinction of this native religious movement.

## The Old Scots Independents

The OSI movement came into being in 1768 but had its forerunners in two Presbyterian ministers in the Borders. One was Henry Davidson, minister in Galashiels, 1724 -1756. The other was Gabriel Wilson who ministered at the same time in nearby Maxton. The two men were close friends and when the 1732 General Assembly restored patronage, they were so disgusted as to renounce their sacramental commission within the Church of Scotland. They continued to teach, preach and baptise but would not administer the Lord's Supper. In 1736, the two organised an independent group in Maxton along congregational lines. This continued for twenty years. It was a most remarkable situation as both men continued in their capacity of ministers of the established church. After their death, the independent congregation kept going and formed ties with the OSI movement. Thomas Boston of Ettrick was a notable forerunner of Davidson and Wilson. His book "Human Nature in its Fourfold State" was very influential. His tombstone at Ettrick reads:

*"The Rev. Thomas Boston Sr. whose private character was highly respectable, whose public labours were blessed to many and whose valuable writings have contributed much to promote the advancement of vital Christianity. Born Duns, 17 March 1676, ordained to pastoral charge of Simperin, September 21 1699, removed to Ettrick May 1 1707 and died May 20 1732, aged 56 leaving a widow and 4 children."*

In 1768, James Smith and Robert Ferrier, ministers of the neighbouring parishes of Newborn and Largo in Fife produced an important publication, 'The Case of James Smith, late minister at Newborn and Robert Ferrier, late minister of Largo truly represented and defended.' Both men were much influenced by the thinking of John Glas. In 1814, their 'Case' was re-published by James McCain of Paisley in 'A Concise Abstract of the Faith, Hope and Practise of the OSI's.' What was their 'Case' against the established church of their day? It was this: they acknowledged, "That the Westminster Confession of Faith contained 'many most precious truths' and 'it is mostly founded upon the Word of God'." However, there were certain doctrines they could not accept:

First, the eternal son ship of Christ. He was not eternally the Son, they said. Second, the eternal progression of the Holy Spirit from Father and Son. Third, saving faith they said was not a complex but a simple act 'an accepting of God's test concerning His Son and a receiving, resting and relying on Him for salvation.' Fourth, the authority of the civil magistrate in ecclesiastical affairs is wrong. Fifth, the power of the civil magistrate to call synods is wrong. Sixth, the power of censure and discipline should rest with church officers not members.

On the other hand, they held to the autonomy of the local church under the leadership of a plurality of elders; no educational stipulation for ministers; the receipt of members by public profession of faith; the Lord's Supper on the first day of every week.

After stating their 'case', the two resigned their ministries and organised an independent church at Balchristie (village of the Christians), Fife in 1768. It was the first of what came to be known as the Old Scots Independent Churches. It soon grew to around seventy members, Smith and Ferrier serving as elders. The second congregation was established in Glasgow when a small group left the Relief Church of William Cruden. They considered Cruden incompetent but the magistrate and the town council would not recognise their choice of minister. They appointed as their leaders three men, Archibald Paterson, Matthew Alexander and David Dale. The latter was the owner the Blantyre cotton mill and founded the New Lanark cotton mill along with his son-in-law, Robert Owen. Denying the Presbyterian form of church government, they met at first in a private house. Then, with a membership of twenty-five, they built a 'chapel' as Independents would refer to their church buildings. It was situated at Greyfriars Wynd, now Shuttle Street, Glasgow. It was referred to as 'the Candle Kirk' as it was built through the generosity of Paterson, a wealthy Glasgow candle maker.

Hearing of the 'Case' of the two Fife ministers, Paterson, Alexander and Dale sent to Balchristie. As a result, Robert Ferrier came to Glasgow where he was installed in the eldership with David Dale. James Smith stayed at Balchristie and James Simpson, a Largo Weaver, was appointed to the eldership with him. David Dale became the first 'layman' to officiate as a minister in a Glasgow church. This attracted much hostility. The windows of the meetinghouse were often shattered by stones. However the movement grew and new congregations were established over the years from 1768 to 1814 at Airdrie, Dundee, Earlsferry, Edinburgh, Galashiels, Hamilton, Kirkcaldy, Marykirk, Methven, Montrose, New Lanark, Newburgh, Paisley, Perth and Sauchieburn. The congregation in Glasgow flourished under the leadership of Dale and Ferrier. David Dale, known as 'the benevolent magistrate', was a remarkable man. He was born at Stewarton in Ayrshire in 1739. His father was a shopkeeper but David became a shepherd before being apprenticed to a Paisley weaver. He then became a shopkeeper and manufacturer. By 1782, he had his own company. In 1783, he was visited by Richard Arkwright, the inventor of the spinning frame. Dale showed him the potential power of the Falls of Clyde and the two became partners. The New Lanark Mills were opened in 1786. By 1793, they were the largest mills in Britain, employing 1300 workers. Dale was a pioneer of industrial welfare. He took in many destitute men, women and children, housing them and training them. Greville Ewing, itinerating through Lanarkshire in 1799, noted that Dale took in about 500 children aged between seven and fourteen from poor houses and the streets. He employed them and taught them reading, writing and principles of religion. They attended the local Secession Church. Dale encouraged many ministers in their preaching. He had a part in building the mill workers' accommodation at Catrine and then Blantyre, from whence came David Livingstone. During his lifetime, it is estimated he gave over £50,000 to charity. For thirty-seven years, he was a pastor at the Greyfriars Wynd congregation. He taught himself Greek and Hebrew to better equip himself and preached every Sunday.

The year 1770 saw a split in the congregation over various differences such as the use of the Lord's Prayer in public worship, whether 'Amen' should be pronounced audibly by the congregation after prayer and whether to stand while singing as well as praying. Dale urged forbearance. Ferrier pressed for 'unity of judgement.' The result was that Ferrier and his party left to join the Glasite Church in Glasgow. Dale continued with his Independent church. It met until 1940, latterly in the Christian Institute of Glasgow. In Paisley, Dale helped in establishing the Abbey Close Independents. Records exist of a similar group in Paisley known as 'the Pend Folk' after their meeting place in the Pend. The congregation was formed in 1796 and reached a peak of 164 members. Later they met in Barr Street before dying out. In 1800, Dale purchased 'Rosebank House' near Cambuslang where he died in March 1806. He was buried in the Ramshorn Churchyard, near Candleriggs, Glasgow. The OSI congregation in Airdrie, established in 1807, only existed for a short time owing to a bitter division over baptism. The congregation in Dundee came into being in 1769 due to the work of Andrew Scott. He had been suspended by the Bell Street Anti-burger Secession Church for his opposition to swearing covenants. The congregation met in Barrack Street. The Earlsferry congregation only came into the OSI fold in 1813. It had been a Haldanite group.

Congregations of the OSI's were never numerous or large. As early as 1776, the subject of believer's baptism caused much controversy and they lost many members to the Scotch Baptists. The OSI's accepted infant baptism. Perhaps the total membership never exceeded 500. In 1814, they formed a union with the Inghamite Congregations of the North of England. Benjamin Ingham had accompanied John Wesley to America but did not become a Methodist. By 1761, the Inghamites had established a separate identity. By 1814, there were thirteen congregations with 252 members. They were Kendal, Nottingham, Bulwell, Tadcaster, Howden, Leeds, Bradford and Wisbey, Todmorden, Salterforth, Ruthwell and Tosside, Wirenall near Colne, Wheatley and Haslingden. New OSI congregations were formed in 1814 at Falkirk and 1837 at Lesmahagow and Glasford. However, by then others were already dying out. A pamphlet produced in 1835 attributed their decline to their non-evangelistic nature and the rise of the Haldanite Churches. Another factor was that like many such groups they could not handle the religious freedom that was now prevalent and were almost by nature self-destructive.

## The Bereans

This movement began at Fettercairn, Kincardineshire in 1773 and continued for seventy years. Its founder was John Barclay. He was born into a farming family at Muthill, Perthshire in 1734 and educated at St Andrews University, graduating in 1755. In 1759, he was licensed by the Presbytery of Auchterarder and he became James Jobson's assistant at Errol. After four years, he was dismissed for teaching 'dangerous doctrines.' In 1763, he became Anthony Dow's assistant at Fettercairn. Dow died in 1772 and Barclay succeeded him at Fettercairn. He became a great preacher. Multitudes came to hear him and people would fill the building, sit on the rafters and stand outside by the windows. In 1766 and 1767, he had published two books, a 'Paraphrase of the Psalms' and 'Rejoice Evermore or Christ in All the Scriptures.' Because of certain 'questionable statements', he was called before the Presbytery of Fordoun. He was dismissed and when he asked for the customary Presbyterial Certificate of Character, it was refused. An appeal to the Synod and the General Assembly was dismissed in 1773.

Cut off from the established church, he formed an independent congregation at Sauchieburn in the parish of Marykirk. Similar groups were formed in Edinburgh and Crieff. James MacRae took over at Sauchieburn in 1774. After three years in Edinburgh meeting in a building in the Cowgate, Barclay was invited to London by friends and readers of his publications. William Nelson took charge of the Edinburgh congregation. 'Berean fellowships' were then established in Glasgow, Stirling, Kirkcaldy, Dundee, Arbroath, Montrose and Brechin. Barclay visited every one of them, travelling on foot. He died on the 29th July 1798 and he was buried in the Old Calton Churchyard, Edinburgh. The ruling principle of his teaching was always 'the perfection and supreme authority of the Scriptures as the sole test of divine truth.' It is probable that he adopted the name 'Bereans' from his practice of constantly searching the Scriptures (Acts 17:11).  He pioneered the use of hymns in worship.  His book 'Rejoice Evermore' contained 196 of his own hymns.

We have few records of the movement.  In 1823, it appears the congregation in Glasgow had 96 members, Stirling 33 and Crieff 8.  In 1843, the Scottish Ecclesiastical Register and National Almanac said the denomination had been in decline for years.  No connections with England survived.  Only four congregations had ordained ministers - Edinburgh, Glasgow, Dundee and Laurencekirk.  Meetings in other places were kept going by deacons.  Congregations were independent.  Ministers were chosen with no regard of human learning.  It is interesting to note that James MacRae ministered at Sauchieburn until it became a Congregational Church in 1809.  MacRae was one of the first ministers in Scotland to conduct a Sunday school.  This Congregational Church existed until about 1950.  At Sauchieburn, behind a private house, the author and his wife found a plaque on the side of a building now used as a barn.  It read:

*"To James McCrae the Berean Reformer who ministered here for 40 years beginning in 1773 and of his successor, the Rev. Thomas McKinnon whose ministry extended over 40 years ending with his death in 1854.  These servants of God, rich in good works, rest from their labours and their works do follow them."*

Berean meetings finally died out, the last being at Laurencekirk in 1844, although William Taylor carried on with a small group in his own barn at Balmain.  The last Bereans in Laurencekirk were two old ladies one of whom upon the other's death said, "Wae's me, when I gang tae the Bereans'll be clean lickett aff."  As a group, they were attacked because their pastors were mainly tradesmen and their members came from the lower echelons of society. However, it is to their credit that wherever Berean congregations existed a taste for religious knowledge and the reading and study of the Bible increased. This was accompanied by a corresponding increase in standards of morality, temperance and general behaviour. The Bereans practised a down-to-earth, homely religion that fitted their day-to-day lives.

## The Haldane Movement

The central characters of 'the Haldane Revival' were two brothers, Robert and James Haldane. The have been called the 'Wesley and Whitfield' of Scotland. First, consider the scene onto which they came. The year 1760 had seen the establishment of the Carron Ironworks and the beginning of the Industrial Revolution. With it came a spirit of secularism, materialism, rationalism and scepticism. The answer of the established church was 'Moderatism.' Moderates propounded the virtues of education, social reform and cultural advancement. Enthusiasm for the Gospel message was lost. The moral and spiritual tone of the nation thus deteriorated. By 1783, church attendance was down considerably. The French Revolution of 1789 added to the problem. The 'Age of Reason,' as Paine had called it, was certainly not an age when the Gospel flourished. Onto this stage stepped the Haldanes.

Robert was born in 1764 and James in 1768. They were of an aristocratic family, the Haldanes of Gleneagles. Their father was a captain of the East India Company and owned estates at Airthrey, near Stirling. (Today Airthrey Castle is part of the campus of the University of Stirling.) He was on the verge of being elected President of the company when he died in 1768. The boys received their first religious education from their mother. When she too died, they were cared for by their grandmother and then an uncle. Later they were sent to the Royal High School of Edinburgh. The year was 1777. They boarded with the rector, Dr. Adam, in Charles Street. Robert then attended the University of Edinburgh before following in his uncle's footsteps and joining the Royal Navy. By 1780, he had joined 'The Monarch' in Portsmouth. James attended the University of Edinburgh from 1781 studying Greek, Latin, mathematics, logic, metaphysics and natural philosophy. At seventeen, he too went to sea with the East India Company, as had his father before him. Robert came out of the navy in 1783, went back to university, travelled and then settled down on the estate at Airthrey for ten years as a country gentleman. By 1794, James was commanding the East India merchant vessel 'Melville Castle' but quite suddenly, he too retired to private life. Robert was shaken out of his lethargy by the French Revolution and he became an active proponent of its virtues. Later he became disillusioned with it and turned to religion, reading a great deal on Christian evidences. James in the meantime was also reading and meditating upon the Word of God. He became acutely aware of God's grace in the Gospel and the need to be born again. Thus, the direction of the lives of the two brothers completely changed. A friend, William Innes of Stirling, told Robert of Carey's missionary efforts in Serampore, India on behalf of the Baptist Church. Robert then decided to sell the Airthrey estate to finance a mission to Bengal, India. He proposed to take the following ministers, William Innes of Stirling, David Bogue of Gosport and Greville Ewing of Lady Glenorchy's, Edinburgh. Additionally, a printer, John Ritchie, would go to set up a press. Robert sought the co-operation of the government and the East India Company but neither was sympathetic to the plan. A popular petition was even circulated. The Church of Scotland was even less helpful. The General Assembly was controlled by the Moderates and the church was in 'the ice-age of Moderatism.' "Were there not heathen at home?" was their retort. So ended the Haldane's first missionary effort but they would answer the Moderates' taunt.

Greville Ewing and Charles Stuart, an Edinburgh physician, had founded 'The Missionary Magazine' in 1796. Soon its circulation reached 6,000. Missionary societies were founded in London in 1795 and in Glasgow and Edinburgh in 1796. It was a time of great awakening. Ministers such as John Erskine, Walter Buchanan and David Black, friends of the Haldanes, were all busy but neither Robert nor James knew which way to go. John Campbell an ironmonger in Edinburgh's Grassmarket stirred up James. He proposed they start a Sunday school in Gilmerton, a colliery village four miles South of Edinburgh. James was enthusiastic. Campbell, concerned about the destitution of the people in Gilmerton, mostly miners, asked Joseph Rate, a student from David Bogue's academy in Gosport to conduct services for a few weeks. Many attended. After two weeks, Rate was called south unexpectedly. There was no preacher. Campbell consulted James Haldane. James suggested John Aikman, then a university student. Aikman would only consent to one Sunday's preaching and if Rate did not return it was agreed that James Haldane would preach. Reluctantly, his first sermon was delivered on the 6th of May 1797. All were impressed with the earnestness and power of his preaching. Similar schools were established around Edinburgh leading to the setting up of 'The Edinburgh Gratis Sabbath School Society' in 1797. James believed this could be accomplished throughout Scotland and so set off with Campbell on his first tour in the spring of that year. It lasted a week. Schools were set up in Glasgow, Paisley and Greenock. Soon sixty schools existed throughout Central Scotland. On the 12th of July 1797, after prayer in the house of David Black in Edinburgh, James, along with Aikman and Rate went on a major tour of the North of Scotland. Their purpose: "to preach the word of life, not to disseminate matters of doubtful disputation or to make converts to this or the other sect; to distribute pamphlets and endeavour to encourage Christians to use their talents, especially in instituting Sunday Schools for the instruction of youth." They preached in every town and large village in the North, going even to Orkney. Their preaching was done in the streets and at market crosses. They distributed 20,000 pamphlets. They spoke to crowds of two, three and four thousand. Tours had been done before by Wesley and Whitfield, Neil Douglas of the Relief Church and Charles Simeon of Cambridge but they were nothing like this. The tour did not finish until November. On the 20th of December 1797 James Haldane, Aikman and friends drew up further plans to take the Gospel to Scotland. The Society for Propagating the Gospel at Home (SPGH) was formed. At the first general meeting on the 1lth of January 1798 a committee of directors was appointed, all laymen. The society was non-sectarian and inter-denominational. Its purpose was simply this, "to make known the Everlasting Gospel of our Lord Jesus Christ."

Robert Haldane preached his first sermon in a barn at Weem near Aberfeldy in April 1798. He was to be the financial mainspring of the society. The SPGH took over from their previous organisation, the Edinburgh Tract Society. Additionally, in 1798, Greville Ewing made a tour of the North and two Secession ministers, William Ballantine and John Cleghorn joined the society and ministered in Caithness. By late 1799 many Presbyterian, Episcopal, Baptist and Congregational ministers were in the field under the SPGH banner. Two classes existed, catechists who organised and superintended Sunday Schools and ministers, like Ewing, who preached. No collections were made or denominational bias given. A letter of instruction admonished the missionaries "to study Scriptural simplicity in your discourses. Those sermons are always most useful which are most simple. Let not your sermon and your prayer be too long. Much better your hearers should wish you had been longer than be wearied till you close. We are disposed to speak longest when we have least to say." By the turn of the century, 40,000 tracts had been distributed. The established clergy complained that the world was going out of its place!

The northwest Highlands had always been a difficult area in which to work due to the preponderance of Gaelic speakers. However, the SPGH sent Gaelic catechists and preachers and they met with considerable success. By 1798, Robert had sold his Airthrey estate. He supported the SPGH entirely. Also in 1798, he purchased 'the Circus' in Little King Street, Edinburgh for a place of worship. John Campbell suggested the idea of a Tabernacle after the plan of Whitfield. Soon Robert financed the scheme. When Rowland Hill, the great English evangelist, came to Scotland he preached to 2,500 people in the Tabernacle. On Sunday evenings the crowd, in excess of 15,000 had to move out onto the Calton Hill. In 1799, Robert bought a building on Jamaica Street, Glasgow for £3,000 and converted it into a Tabernacle. Similar meeting places were secured in Dundee, Perth, Elgin, Thurso, Wick, Dunkeld and Dumfries. They were not intended as new denominations but simply as places for the preaching of the Gospel. The idea met with such success that local alehouses had to close down on Sundays, the crowds having gone to the Tabernacle!

Thus far, the Haldanes were still members of the established church, the Church of Scotland, but thought of the desirability of constituting an independent church. Greville Ewing had withdrawn from the established church. An SPGH meeting in December 1798 considered the matter. The result was they decided to form an independent church. Ewing attended to how the church should be governed. Its format was to be congregational in nature. James Haldane was invited to be the first preacher. In January 1799, the congregation came into being with 272 members. A new Tabernacle was built on Leith Walk. Greville Ewing became 'pastor' to the Glasgow Tabernacle and William Innes to the Dundee Tabernacle. Like Ewing, Innes had resigned as a minister of the Church of Scotland. In the meantime, Robert had established a seminary to train young men for the ministry. It ran for ten years. Classes were conducted in Edinburgh, Glasgow, Dundee, Elgin and Grantown. Nearly 300 preachers were trained. Robert invested £80,000.

What about the life and faith of these Haldanite congregations? Like the Scotch Baptists, they accepted the weekly observance of the Lord's Supper. Strict discipline was maintained. Members were examined as to their Bible knowledge and purity of life. The movement was soon rejected by the Church of Scotland, which refused to allow its ministers to have anything to do with the Haldanes. Within the movement, a division occurred over the subject of baptism. Some members, recognising the place and purpose of baptism in God's plan, took a very strong stand. James urged forbearance. However, on reading Archibald McLean's 'Review of Dr Wardlaw's

Lectures on Infant Baptism' James himself was baptised in March 1808. Ironically, a month earlier he had called a student, Lachlan Macintosh, to account for preaching in support of baptism. Macintosh had been immersed in a Scotch Baptist meetinghouse. Later that same year Robert was also baptised, as were over 200 members of the church. Most of the rest, who did not accept baptism, withdrew and formed themselves in to a church along Congregational lines meeting in Barnard's Rooms, West Thistle Street, Edinburgh. William Innes was ordained as pastor. Similar splits occurred elsewhere. In Glasgow, about forty joined the Scotch Baptists. The rest formed a Congregational Church and their pastor was Greville Ewing. Later in Glasgow, he met a young man, Alexander Campbell, who had been shipwrecked on Islay while undertaking a voyage to America. He introduced Campbell to the Haldanes while he studied at Glasgow University during 1808 and Campbell was greatly influenced by them. He in turn had a great influence on the Restoration Movement in America after a more successful voyage of emigration in 1809.

Division over the question of baptism continued and affected Haldanite groups in Perth, Wick, Arbroath, Falkirk and other places. Robert settled at Auchengray near Airdrie in 1809 and formed a congregation. James continued his preaching tours until 1829. Some church historians take the view that the Haldane movement crystallised in 1843 as the Free Church of Scotland. There is no doubt that this great native phenomenon was influenced by earlier movements such as the Glasites. Its successors are more doubtful. The success of the Haldane revival has been explained in terms of the following reasons: a conducive climate of the public mind; the ineffectuality of the churches particularly the national Church of Scotland; the liberality of Robert Haldane; the spiritual fervour and energy of the missionaries; the firm grip of evangelistic theory of the Haldanes and the training of young preachers.

Consider briefly Robert's training programme. In a letter to John Campbell of the 6th of October 1798, he stated the origin and aim of his theological seminary: "I intend to give one year's education to ten or twelve persons of any age that may be fit for it, under Mr Bogue, with a view to the ministry." This was accomplished with students being sent south to Mr Bogue at Gosport. Greville Ewing was entrusted with the first class in January 1799. Twenty-four students, mainly of Presbyterian background, were enrolled. They went into the field in November 1800. In January 1800, the second class spent a year under the direction of William Innes at Dundee before finishing with a year at Glasgow with Greville Ewing. The class numbered over fifty. Aikman, Campbell, Wemyss, Stephens, Cowie and Walker all tutored until the seminary finished in December 1808. By that time, it had served a great purpose in putting over 300 men into the field. During this time, Robert paid students' board, medical expenses, tuition and books. He gave them an allowance of £54 over two years. The subjects taught were English grammar and rhetoric, Greek, Hebrew, systematic theology and on request, Latin, French and church music. In their annual break, students were sent out to work with congregations.

Significantly, Haldanite congregations were established in America. They were known as Haldane churches. When Walter Scott of Moffat, not the famous writer but the Restoration preacher, left Scotland and with it the Presbyterian religion of his family, he came to a Haldane church in Pittsburgh, Pennsylvania led by George Forrester, another immigrant Borderer from Ayton. Indeed, Scott was immersed into Christ by Forrester in the year 1818. Around that time, there were Haldane churches in some of the other major cities of the United States such as New York, Boston, Philadelphia and Baltimore. This was significant in that the ideas of the Haldanes, who influenced pioneers like Alexander Campbell and who in turn, had been influenced by the likes of John Glas, Robert Sandeman and others, crossed the Atlantic and would contribute mightily to the Restoration Movement in 'the New World.'

If James was the popular preacher, Robert was the scholar. He lectured on Bible exposition in Geneva and Montauban. His students included Malan, Monod and D'Aubigne. The latter wrote, "If Geneva gave something to Scotland at the time of the Reformation, Geneva has received something in return in the blessed exertions of Robert Haldane." His favourite subjects were the great doctrines of salvation by grace, justification by faith and forgiveness through the cross of Christ. His commentary on Romans remains a classic.

Robert died in 1842. His brother commented, "He preceded me in Christ, now he has preceded me into glory." James died a few years later in 1851. Truly, the contribution of Robert and James Haldane was immense.

**PART THREE**

–

**RESTORATION: A WORLD IDEAL**

# CHAPTER 6

# THE RESTORATION MOVEMENT

## The Early Period 1800 - 1847

After three centuries of religious upheaval, the nineteenth century was graced by the fruit of this vast amount of study and debate. The conclusion of the matter for many was simple: man could do no better than return to the purity of Christian doctrine as delivered by Christ and preached by His apostles. So many movements had arisen which, though sharing much in common, also had so many differences, that many religious people turned their back on denominational creeds and sectarian confessions of faith to return to the pure Christianity of New Testament times with its great vitality and unity. These groups took one of the names ascribed to God's people in the New Testament, Churches of Christ. They arose throughout the British Isles.

At Auchtermuchty in Fife in 1809 thirteen members of an Independent church formed on Haldanite principles were immersed into Christ after the New Testament order in the River Eden. The leaders were the brothers John and George Dron. The group remained independent as a Church of Christ. In 1834, John Dron visited similar groups in the USA led by Alexander Campbell. In a private house in Cox Lane, Allington, Denbighshire, in the same year another such Church of Christ came into being. The leader, Charles Davies, was immersed into Christ in a Baptist building in Wrexham and returned to immerse over thirty others. John Davies became the preacher. It was not until 1835 that they learned of other such congregations in Britain and the USA. In Dunganon, Ireland in 1810 the leader of an Independent church, Robert Tener, was immersed along with his wife and the brothers William and Robert Smith. Together they formed a Church of Christ.

In the Furness Peninsula of Cumbria there was a congregation meeting in a small chapel built about 1826. Its origin was older. It was 'discovered' in 1854 and later William Robinson in an unpublished paper 'History of the Church in Furness' wrote, "This Church undoubtedly owes its origin to a group of churches of similar though not identical faith and order which began their troubled history in the troubled days after the restoration of Charles II. There were at least four of these churches and three have now ceased to exist. The fourth, Tottlebank, is now in the Baptist Union. Fortunately, it possessed a minute book going back to its foundation in 1669. The church minute book contains a full confession of faith and it is interesting to note that the church had the following marks usually associated with the reformation of the Campbells: It was named 'the Church of Christ.' Only believer's baptism by immersion was practised. The Lord's Supper was the chief service of worship each Sunday and only baptised communicants were allowed. The government was congregational and there was liberty of ministry. Elders and Deacons were ordained and one elder served as 'teaching elder' and was supported by the Church." The church at Kirby separated from the group when the latter adopted 'open communion' and remained isolated until 1854. Other such churches came into being in such places as Wrexham, Shrewsbury, Grangemouth, Newmilns and London. From these small beginnings in the early nineteenth century, the movement accelerated. One story especially bears repeating. William Jones, a bookseller who had moved from Liverpool to London in 1800 became a pastor of the Scotch Baptist congregation in Windmill Street. In 1833 a young American, Peyton C. Wyeth, studying art in Europe visited Jones' congregation. He told of 'the current reformation' in the USA. From the description given, Jones concluded the order of public worship was very close to that of the Scotch Baptists. He asked for the name of some of the American leaders that he might correspond. He contacted Alexander Campbell and received his papers 'The Christian Baptist' and 'The Millenial Harbinger.' From 1835, he published these for sixteenth months in Britain. He then ceased publication due to doctrinal differences. However, he published enough to cause much thought on the subject.

In March 1837 James Wallis, a Nottingham draper and Scotch Baptist began to publish his 'Christian Messenger and Reformer.' By August, a congregation of sixty-two existed after the New Testament pattern. Wallis continued to edit the Christian Messenger for twenty-five years. By 1840, it reported New Testament churches in Newark, Glasgow, Dundee, Perth, Banff, Turriff, Liverpool, Newcastle-upon-Tyne, Lincoln, Edinburgh, Cupar, Dunfermline, Montrose, Dumfries, Chester and Banbury. In both Great Britain and the USA, these Churches of Christ shared the same principles: a great desire for Christian unity, an aim to restore New Testament Christianity, to use and be known by Bible names, opposition to creeds, the doctrine of conversion (faith, repentance, confession and baptism) the Lord's Supper weekly and the Church order of elders, deacons and evangelists.

In 1839 G.C. Reid, minister of an independent evangelical Church in Dundee was baptised with over a hundred of his congregation. In July 1840, he began a ten-month tour visiting Cupar, Auchtermuchty, Alva, Dunfermline, Glasgow, Dumfries and Carlisle. After a few months rest he made a second tour of five months visiting Dunfermline, Glasgow, Dumfries, Carlisle, Chester, Wrexham, Wigan, Nottingham, Newark, Lincoln, Horncastle, London, Fraserburgh and Banff. On the 18th and 19th of August 1842 at the South Bridge Hall, Edinburgh forty young Churches of Christ met and reported the following statistics:

England had 19 congregations with 530 members

Wales had 3 congregations with 95 members

Scotland had 21 congregations with 608 members

The largest congregations: Nottingham, 202; Edinburgh, 94; Cupar, 91 and Dundee, 70.

Early in 1843, William Thompson of Edinburgh became the second evangelist to work with the new congregations. While still a Scotch Baptist, he had spent two years in London and Leeds and he was a member in London when P.C. Wyeth visited. As an evangelist, in a three-month tour, he visited Bathgate, Airdrie, Kilmarnock, Newmilns, Glasgow, Saltcoats, Lanark, Sanquar and Galashiels. In March 1844, after a few months with the congregation in Edinburgh, George Greenwell of Bedlington became the third evangelist. 'The Restoration Movement,' as it would be known, was launched.

## The Middle Period 1848 - 1914

In any movement, the initial stages are usually vibrant and exciting. Staying the course is more difficult. It takes tenacity and perseverance. In the early years of the Restoration Movement William Thompson noted that the efforts of the evangelists were spread too thin and that more ministers of the Word were needed. The only way that the young churches saw to remedy this situation was to pool their resources. At first this was tried nationally and then at a district level. Evangelists were supported by groups of churches and they would divide their time among them, ministering to each in turn. This seemed like a good arrangement but in later years proved a dangerous concept as all sorts of supra-congregational committees evolved to take care of the business of the church. This jeopardised the New Testament principle of congregational autonomy. Matters that should have rested with elders and members of local churches were taken out of their hands. They were then dealt with by a multiplicity of select groups that functioned above the level of the local churches. The other means that was tried to gain evangelists was an appeal to brethren in the USA, especially to Alexander Campbell's Bethany College, a training school for preachers in Virginia. In 1847, Campbell and James Henshaw spent a few months touring in England, Scotland and Ireland. The tour was not without problems. Within the church, there was a debate over 'open' or 'closed' communion (whether non-Christians should be allowed to partake of the Lord's Supper). Campbell took a position that may be stated as 'neither invite nor debar.' British churches practised closed communion. Out-with the church, the problem was the issue of slavery. Wilberforce's Emancipation of Slavery Bill had become law in 1833 but in America, the slavery issue would not be resolved until the Civil War of

Abraham Lincoln's day (1865). Campbell held slaves. In Scotland, the Rev. Robertson of the Scottish Anti-slavery Society even had Campbell imprisoned in Duke Street gaol, Glasgow over the issue. Later he was totally exonerated. Before he returned to the USA, he chaired the second general meeting of Churches of Christ in Great Britain. This second conference was attended by representatives of thirteen English congregations, seven Scottish, five Welsh and one Irish. The records were encouraging. In 1842, fifty congregations reported a membership of 1300. In 1847, eighty congregations reported 2300 members. Most encouraging was the prayerful and zealous concern for the Restoration Movement. Every man and woman was a preacher of restoration. Churches strove for pure teaching and practical Christian living. Of concern was the practice of 'mutual ministry,' which encouraged every brother to take up the right to preach or speak publicly, sometimes irrespective of ability. Also of concern was the non-evangelistic nature of the church, which had been inherited from the Glasites and the Scotch Baptists. The major influences in the formative early period (1800-1847) had been men such as William Jones, James Wallis and Alexander Campbell. The middle period, dated 1848-1914, should have been extremely fruitful but it did not meet with unqualified success. Indeed, it witnessed a great deal of confusion and disruption. Campbell was unable to find even one evangelist to aid the Restoration cause in Britain. In 1848, Dr. Thomas came and toured for two years. He was an ex-disciple and an energetic though troublesome man. All he brought to Britain was the erroneous teaching of Christadelphianism. He caused problems wherever he went. This was especially so in Scotland. Seven congregations were destroyed including all those in Ayrshire. Others such as Edinburgh, Glasgow and Cupar were weakened both numerically and spiritually. There were no evangelists to meet the challenge of Thomas and the sad episode turned many congregations against fellowship with American congregations. So too did the activities of the American church's Foreign Missionary Society in sending F.W. Moore to Liverpool in 1875. It showed a disregard and lack of understanding for native evangelistic efforts in England.

However many native men did come to the fore and they made immense contributions to the Restoration Movement in the British Isles. Among the most notable were David King who worked in London and Birmingham. He was a tireless and talented worker throughout the second half of the nineteenth century. Francis Hill of Sunderland was another great worker. J.B. Rotherham was a scholar of immense stature. He worked chiefly in Wales although his translation of the Bible made an impact throughout the world. In Liverpool, the influence of two brothers H.E. and G.Y. Tickle was tremendous. Many of their songs are still used in songbooks today. In Scotland, one of the most able men was Thomas Hughes Milner. The congregations where these men ministered numbered their memberships in the hundreds. They were strongholds of truth and zeal. Their influence stretched throughout the land. Towards the close of the nineteenth century, other men of great ability emerged. Lancelot Oliver succeeded David King as a great writer, orator and editor. In the north of England, Timothy Coop and in London, Sidney Black and R.K. Francis fulfilled good ministries as evangelists. Charles Abercrombie and James Anderson did the same in Scotland. Many other able men also graced the movement and were a credit to that for which they stood. Their influence was not limited to these islands but stretched right around the world. Christians from these shores took the Restoration Movement to Canada, Australia, New Zealand and other parts of the British Empire.  Missionaries went out to Africa and Asia.  While preparing this material the writer had the privilege of speaking to two elderly sisters in the town of Stonehouse, Scotland.  They were the daughters of the first British missionary to Burma, Robert Halliday.

The energy and talent that went into the movement was so immense it is an injustice to reduce it to a set of statistics.  Nevertheless, consider these figures for evangelism:

From 1855-65 membership increased from 2,000 to 4,000, 100% growth.

From 1865-75 membership increased from 4,000 to 5,000, 25% growth.

From 1875-85 membership increased from 5,000 to 7,500, 50% growth.

From 1885-95 membership increased from 7,500 to 10,500, 40% growth.

In 1874, 15 evangelists were working with 4,400 members in 109 congregations.  Various publications were put out during the period 1835-1900:

The Millenial Harbinger, the Christian Messenger and Reformer, the Ecclesiastical Observer, the Bible Advocate, the Gospel Banner and Biblical Treasury, the Christian Advocate, The Open Door and the Sunbeam.  The level of publication reflects the vitality of the movement.  No training school existed however until 1920 when Overdale College at Selly Oak, Birmingham was founded.  We now come to this later period of development, 1900-1945.

## The Later Period 1915 - 1945

This period saw vast and irreversible changes in the world as two great wars were fought out across the globe. The church too faced great change. Two generations of young Christian men and women had to face up to the issue of going off to war. At home, the church continued to grow. In 1890, 146 churches reported 8,985 members. In 1900, 173 churches reported 11,789 members. In 1911, 200 churches reported 14,725 members. In 1923, 201 churches reported 16,465 members. In 1939, 176 churches reported 15,229 members. This period however saw a movement back towards the denominational world. The 1914 conference agreed to join the Faith and Order Movement and sent representatives to their conference in Geneva in 1920. Publications abounded from songbooks to tracts. From 1935 the leading magazine was the Scripture Standard, the first editor being Walter Crosswaite. From its beginning in the opening years of the nineteenth century, the Restoration Movement now numbered congregations after the New Testament pattern in 41 countries of the world with a membership of nearly two million.

At home however, apathy, seen in the lack of evangelistic effort, and false teaching, seen in liberalism and modernism, caused the movement to lose its way and its identity. Many Churches of Christ went out of existence or merged with other religious groups such as Methodists or Baptists. Eventually a large part of the movement became part of the United Reform Church in 1980. What began as a bold effort to restore New Testament Christianity ended in denominationalism. Only a small remnant remained. It was time for a new beginning.

# CHAPTER 7

# NEW TESTAMENT CHRISTIANITY

## The Lord's Church - a New Birth

For the birth of the Church of Christ, we must look to the second chapter of the book of Acts. The expression 'New Testament Christianity' is used to specify apostolic Christianity, as it existed in the first century. Can any other kind of Christianity be considered as valid? However, in terms of Scotland, we shall now look at what may be considered as a new birth.

The immediate post-war period saw the surviving Churches of Christ at low ebb. However in the 1950's new steps forward were taken. The Restoration plea of a return to New Testament Christianity had to be sounded again. Men such as Walter Crossthwaite had carried the banner valiantly. It was taken over by men such as Will Steele, David Dougal, Len Channing, Raymond Hill, Philip Partington, Frank Worgan, Andrew Gardiner, Albert Winstanley and Joe Nisbet. In order to be more effective ministers of the Word, most of these men gave up their chosen vocations. Others, too numerous to mention and generally unknown to this author remained in their field of work but nevertheless did a great job in the churches. All of these did a marvellous work not only in establishing new congregations but also in reviving and promoting the Restoration cause. A new vigour and vitality was to be found in the young congregations which came into existence during this period. A new generation of men came forward to do the work of evangelists. Many were native men. Others came from sister congregations in the USA. Together they formed a bond that resulted in much good and lasting work being accomplished in many places. In Scotland, something of the progress of this new Restoration Movement is seen in the establishment of new congregations. Prior to 1950 there were the older congregations such as Kirkcaldy and Slamannan, established as a result of the original Restoration Movement. To this were added the new congregations: in the 1950's, Hyvot's Bank in Edinburgh, in the 1960's, Castlemilk in Glasgow and Sighthill in Edinburgh in the 1970's, Easthouses, Glenrothes, East Kilbride, Dunoon and Clarkston in Glasgow, in the 1980's Aberdeen, Inverness, Livingston, Irvine, Dundee, Ayr, Cumbernauld, Perth, Stirling and Clydebank. More younger men have come forward to do the work of evangelists, contemporaries of this writer, and we must leave it to future church historians to write about their work. What those historians will record will be based on what is done by those of us who hold dear the concept of a return to New Testament Christianity. We do not know what the 21st century will hold but we look forward to the future with an optimism based on a solid foundation of expansion and a faith in Him who holds all things in His hands.

# CONCLUSION

It is most certainly the case that when falling away from God's truth occurs the way of return is always harder than the way of departure. Building up is harder than tearing down. Sometimes even the very foundations seem to be obscured. It is also sad to note that most departures begin with good intentions. However, thank God for His marvellous Word, the Bible. There, for all generations, is the wisdom of Heaven for the woes of Earth. Therein is revealed God's plan for His Church. If we take hold of that Word, never letting it go, respecting its authority and submitting all things to its testing we can, in any age, restore that which was built by Christ and the apostles in the first century. That is important. Men go on building their own religious organisations at peril of their own salvation. Check the warnings of the Scriptures.

This work has attempted to trace the struggle for truth throughout several centuries in Europe, Britain and Scotland. In doing this, we must be aware of the influence of ideas from elsewhere. It is only in this fascinating historical interplay that progress was made. We began in Pre-Reformation times by noting the corrupt state and corrupting influence of the Medieval Roman Church. From there, the struggle for truth, the aspiration to reach out for that which is purer and nobler, had its beginning. We saw first the shattering force of the Reformation and the Presbyterian system being established as the national religion of Scotland in the second half of the sixteenth century. In the seventeenth century, we noted the important influence of non-conformism. This was mainly achieved by Cromwellian troops at the time of the Commonwealth (1650-60). Here Brethren, Quaker, Puritan and Anabaptist influences were introduced into Scotland. In the eighteenth century in a far more enlightened and liberal society, Independency made its mark. The times allowed for the existence of other religious groups besides the established church. This would never have been tolerated two centuries earlier. Even within Presbyterianism, we saw the rise of the Secession Church, the Relief Church and the Free Church. Out-with Presbyterianism the successors to seventeenth century non-conformism appeared - the Glasites, the Keiss Church, the Scotch Baptists, the Old Scots Independents, the Bereans and the Haldane Movement. In the nineteenth century, we saw the impact of the Restoration Movement in the establishment of independent churches that sought to re-establish the faith and practise of the Church of New Testament times. These took the name Disciples of Christ or, more commonly, Churches of Christ. Although the fruit was borne in the nineteenth century, let no one make the mistake of thinking that the movement suddenly sprung up at this time. Rather it was the culmination of centuries of thought, ideas and work. Similarly, the locations in which Churches of Christ arose were neither arbitrary nor co-incidental. In the background, there is always an idea, an influence, a man representing the truth. Sometimes we cannot discover this background story whilst in other instances it is apparent. For example, why should a Church of Christ appear in the little Scottish border town of Galashiels? Pure chance? No! The answer lies in the influence of men like Henry Davidson and Gabriel Wilson. Why have Churches of Christ always had strong roots in Fife? Mere co-incidence? No! The answer lies in the influence of men such as John Glas, James Smith and Robert Ferrier. How did Churches of Christ come to be established in the fishing communities of the northeast? The answer lies in the tours of men such as James Haldane, James Watt and G.C. Reid. What influences led to Churches of Christ appearing in Edinburgh and Glasgow? The answer lies with men such as Robert Sandeman, Robert Carmichael and Archibald McLean. All of these either worked towards or laid the foundation of 'the Restoration Principle.' It may be stated simply in this way, 'back to the Bible.' That is what these men and a host of others strove to achieve. We are blessed to be heirs of that legacy but more so, we are blessed to be heirs of the Word of God itself and this alone, without anything else, has the power to instruct us in the paths of salvation.

One more cautionary word. Let us not fall into another trap, namely that of thinking that because the Church of New Testament times has been restored we can sit back and relax. In the first place, has it been fully restored? The question is asked to prompt every reader to make the inquiry 'has Christ authorised and would he recognise and approve of the religion which I practise?' In the second place, restoration, having been accomplished is never thereby secured for all generations. It is the responsibility of each generation to teach the next. However, it is the responsibility of each generation to check all things with the Word of God. A second hand faith, believing because our parents believed, is no good. Neither does one generation's faithfulness assure the faithfulness of the next. Do not make that assumption. That has happened in the past with disastrous consequences. We cannot guarantee faithfulness in generations to come. We can do our best to pass on a sound religious heritage and point them to that which will never let them down, the Word of God.

To future generations this - accept nothing because it is said by an older generation, that is traditionalism. Take the Bible as your guide in all things. Examine, evaluate and apply then re-examine, re-evaluate and re-apply. Make the faith your own. Only in this way can you have that which God wants you to have in Christ. Then and only then can we all come to know God and the salvation He has provided in Christ. Then and only then will we be able to dwell together in the presence of God throughout all eternity. Ultimately, that is all that counts.

The Reformation and the Restoration are usually thought of as separate movements. Historians tend to 'compartmentalise'. However, let us remember that the things we have seen were the attempts of men and women to serve God aright. Let us consider this great surging tide of religious activity. We owe a great debt of gratitude to those who pursued the quest. We owe it to ourselves to pursue that quest. We owe those who come after us a sound religious heritage. In this great quest may God bless you. To Him be the glory.

# APPENDIX 1

## Important Dates in the Radical Reformation

1517 - Martin Luther introduces ideas for reform in Augsburg and southern Germany.

1518 - Huldreich Zwingli begins preaching reform in Zurich.

1521 - Luther breaks with the Roman Catholic Church.

1521 - Thomas Munzer leaves the Saxony of the Zwickau prophets for Switzerland.

1522 - In Zurich groups of young religious reformers meet for Bible study and prayer.

1522 - Conrad Grebel and Felix Manz become leaders.

1522 - A new movement is formed called Brethren, Anabaptists by opponents.

1522 - The radical reformers conflict with the state churches of Luther and Zwingli.

1524 - In Zurich the radical reformers break with Zwingli.

1525 - Dissenters are baptised by immersion in the river (21st January).

It is October 31st 1517 in Wittenberg, Germany. A former Augustinian monk now a theologian at the university, Martin Luther, nails his 95 thesis to the door of the church building. The Reformation is underway. In 1518 a Swiss priest, Huldreich Zwingli, begins the Reformation in Zurich. By 1521, Luther separates from the Roman Catholic Church. By 1522, in Zurich groups of younger reformers meet in groups for Bible study and prayer. Their leaders are Conrad Grebel and Felix Manz. They form a new movement which begins within the new Reformation but which soon has to become independent of the reformed church of Zwingli. They conflict with the churches of Luther and Zwingli over issues such as the relationship of church and state, the Lord's Supper and baptism.

1525 - Their views now permeate the Zurich area. Grebel tries to influence Zwingli. Zwingli tolerates them but increasingly regards them as radicals.

Grebel, rejected by Zwingli, turns to pastor Wilhelm Rublin of Zollikon and Louis Herzer. They form an independent congregation within the great church. The means of assembling this congregation is a new baptism of true believers, not infants.

The Council holds a public discussion. Anabaptists refuse to yield. Laws are passed against them. Some are imprisoned. Foreigners are banished. They maintain their testimony - "Not by words alone but with our blood are we ready to bear testimony to the truth of our cause".

Grebel is immersed in River Sitter near St Gall, much to the consternation of Zwingli. They are then joined by George Jacob of Coire. He will be the great evangelist of the movement and is named Blaurock because of his blue cloak. Anabaptists see this as the struggle between the Word of God and the word of Zwingli.

1525 - 1528 the movement spreads and takes a strong hold in Germany especially around Strasburg and Augsburg.

In Zurich, it continues to grow and not only questions infant baptism but also tithing, which supports churches and schools. Zwingli, the reformer, baulks at this but Anabaptists press on. They do not recognise civil authority, which they see as pagan and not of God. They teach that Christians cannot hold public office or bear arms. Thus, society itself is threatened and rises up to eject what it sees as destructive elements. Manz is drowned on the 5th of January 1527. Blaurock is scourged with Rods in Zurich. Two years later, he is burned by Roman Catholics in the Tyrol.

1527 - Anabaptists arrived in Berne. They clamour for more and more reform but the Reformation could not reform every error in two years.

1529 - The Diet of Speier says that Anabaptists should be put to death. Two thousand perish.

1530 Luther urges "the use of the sword against them by right of law" but still the movement spreads and Anabaptist ideas travel down the Rhine and arrive in northern Germany and Holland. They also take root in Moravia.

1534 - Non-pacifist Anabaptists capture the city of Munster. They are put down and widespread persecution begins against Anabaptists of all shades.

1536 - a Roman Catholic priest in Holland joins the movement. His name is Menno Simons. His followers come to be known as Mennonites. Balthaser Hubmaier becomes a leader of the movement in Prague.

By the 1690's the movement has grown slack in the practice of church discipline. Jacob Ammann, a Swiss Mennonite advocates true discipline (shunning). His followers become known as the Amish. Jacob Hutter shepherded the Brethren in Moravia in early years. His followers become known as Hutterites. The original Anabaptist witness continues today in the Menonite, Amish and Hutterite churches. As a result of emigration the movement survives in the new world - the Mennonites throughout the USA, the Amish in the north-eastern USA and the Hutterites in Canada (mostly Manitoba and Alberta).

Definitions:

Palatinate – a province in southwest Germany (mid-Rhine valley) around Heidelberg.

Moravia – a province in eastern Czech Republic. Around Brno and Ostrava

Bohemia – a province in western Czech Republic around Prague

# APPENDIX 2

### Important Dates in Scottish History

1520 The struggle for reform begins in Scotland

1525 Martin Luther's writings arrive in Scotland

1527 Tyndale's New Testament translation is smuggled into Scotland

1528 Martyrdom of Patrick Hamilton by Archbishop Beaton

1530 'The burning time', strong Roman Catholic persecution of Reformers

1540 George Wishart banished by Archbishop James Beaton

1546 Montrose burned at the stake. Beaton murdered

1547 Knox enters St Andrews. Banished to serve as French galley slave

1551 Knox flees from Berwick to Frankfurt and Geneva

1559 Knox returns to Scotland. The Reformation is established

1560 Presbyterian Church of Scotland established

1584 Robert Browne expelled from Scotland for preaching congregationalism

1585 John Penry (Congregationalist) martyred

1603 Union of the Crowns - James I

1611 King James (Authorised) version of the Bible

1637 National Covenant upholding Presbyterianism

1650 Oliver Cromwell's troops in Scotland after execution of Charles I

1651 Solemn League and Covenant opposing Episcopacy

1632 Congregations of Anabaptists established

1660 Commonwealth troops leave Scotland after restoration of Charles II

1661 Royal proclamation against Anabaptists and Quakers

1689 The Glorious Revolution and accession of William and Mary

1707 Union of the Parliaments

1725 Glasite Church led by John Glas

1730 deposition of John Glas from Church of Scotland

1732 expulsion of the Erskines from the Church of Scotland

1733 Secession Church established by the Erskines

1742 revival meetings of English evangelist George Whitfield

1750 Sir William Sinclair and the Church at Keiss

1761 Relief Church established in opposition to patronage

1765 establishment of Scotch Baptist church. Carmichael & McLean

1768 establishment of Old Scots Independents. Smith & Ferrier

1773 establishment of Berean fellowships by John Barclay

1796 beginning of the Haldane revival

1804 Churches of Christ established after New Testament order (Restoration Movement)

# APPENDIX 3

## Summary of Important Movements
## in Scottish Church History

1560 Presbyterian Church of Scotland is established in Scotland as the National Church

1725 the first Glasite congregation came into being and the first Glasite building in 1730

1733 the Secession Church broke away from the Church of Scotland

1750 the church at Keiss, an early independent congregation was formed

1761 the Relief Church was formed to give the people relief from patronage

1765 the Scotch Baptist Church was formed by Carmichael and McLean

1768 the Old Scots Independents were formed by Smith and Ferrier

1773 the Bereans were formed and led by Barclay

1796 the Haldanite Revival came into being led by Robert and James Haldane

1800 the restoration Movement leads to the emergence of Churches of Christ

# APPENDIX 4

## Churches of Christ resulting
## from the Restoration Movement in Scotland

Being a list of places in Scotland where congregations after the New Testament order were established from the beginning of the Restoration Movement in 1800.

Aberchirder, Aberdeen, Alva, Armadale, Airdrie, Auchterarder, Auchtermuchty, Annan, Ayr.

Banff, Bathgate, Blackridge, Bellshill, Boness, Buckhaven, Buckie.

Cupar, Crossgates, Chapelhall, Cairnie, Carluke, Coatbridge, Collin, Cowdenbeath, Craigston, Crofthead, Cardenden, Coaltown.

Dumfries, Dundee, Dunfermline, Dennyloanhead, Dunbar, Dornoch, Dalkeith.

Edinburgh.

Fraserburgh, Findochty, Falkirk.

Glasgow, Grangemouth.

Haddington, Hamilton.

Kilmarnock, Kirkcaldy, Kilwinning, Kilbirnie, Kelty.

Lochgelly, Leslie, Leith.

Montrose, Motherwell, Musselburgh.

New Pitsligo, Newburgh, Newton Stewart, Newmilns, Newtongrange, New Cumnock.

Perth, Peterhead, Pittenweem, Portknockie, Portsoy.

St Andrews, Slamanan, Standburn, Sanquar.

Tranent, Turriff.

West Calder, Whitburn, Wilsontown.

# BIBLIOGRAPHY

Allen, C. Leonard and Hughes, Richard T.  Discovering Our Roots: The Ancestry of Churches of Christ, Abilene Christian University Press, Abilene, Texas, 1988.

Anderson, James.  An Outline of My Life, Publishing Committee of Churches of Christ, Birmingham, England, 1912.

Bede, the Venerable.  The Ecclesiastical History of the English People, Oxford University Press, Oxford, 1994.

Brown, P. H.  Scotland: A Short History, W.H. Meikle, Edinburgh, 1951.

Campbell, Selina H.  Home Life and Reminiscences of A. Campbell, John Burns Publishing Co, St. Louis, Missouri.

Collins, Michael & Price, Matthew.  The Story of Christianity, Dorling Kindersley, London, 1999.

Cooper, Bill.  After the Flood, New Wine Press, Chichester, England, 1995.

Cox, John D.   Church History, Dehoff Publications, Murfreesboro, Tennessee, 1978.

Cunningham, J.   The Church History of Scotland, Edinburgh, 1859.

Dowley, Tim (Gen. Ed.).  The History of Christianity, Lion Publishing, Tring, Hertfordshire, 1977.

Escott, Harry.   History of Scottish Congregationalism, Congregational Union of Scotland, Glasgow, 1960.

Estep, William R.   The Anabaptist Story, William B. Eerdmans Publishing Company, Grand Rapids, Michigan, 1975.

Ferguson, Everett.   Church History Reformation and Modern, Biblical Research Press, Abilene, Texas, 1967.

Ford, Harold W.  A History of the Restoration Plea, College Press, Joplin, Missouri, 1952

Garrison, W.E. & DeGroot, A.T.  The Disciples of Christ, A History, Standard Publishing, Cincinnati, Ohio.

Gatherwood, Christopher.   Crash Course on Church History, Hodder and Stoughton, London, 1998.

Grafton, Thomas W.   Alexander Campbell, Christian Publishing Co, St. Louis, 1897

Haldane, Alexander.   The Lives of Robert and James Haldane, The Banner of Truth Trust, Edinburgh, 1990.

Hoad, Jack. The Baptist, Grace Publications Trust, London, 1886.

Hudson, John Allen.  The Church of Christ in Great Britain, Old Paths book Club, London, 1948.

Ker, John.   The Erskines: Ebenezer and Ralph, James Gemmell, Edinburgh, 1881.

King, Louise.  Memoir of David King, Restoration Reprint Library, College Press, Joplin, Missouri, n.d.

Klingman, George A.  Church History for Busy People, Gospel Advocate Company, Nashville, n.d.

Longan, G.W.  The Origin of the Disciples of Christ, Christian Publishing Co, St. Louis, 1889.

McMillon, Lynn.  Restoration Roots, Hester Publications, Henderson, Tennessee, 1983.

Mattox, F.W. The Eternal Kingdom,Gospel Light Publishing Company, Delight, Arkansas, 1961.

Moore, W.T.  A Comprehensive History of the Disciples of Christ, Fleming H. Revell Co. New York, 1909.

Moore, W.T.   The Life of Timothy Coop, Standard Publishing, Cincinnati, Ohio.

Murch, James DeForest.   Christians Only, Standard Publishing, Cincinnati, Ohio, 1962.

Nolt, Steven M.  A History of the Amish, Good Books, Intercourse, Pennsylvania, 1992.

Powell, J.M.  The Cause We Plead, 20th Century Christian, Nashville, 1987.

Richardson, Robert.  Memoirs of Alexander Campbell, Religious Book Service, Indianapolis, Indiana, 1897.

Ross, James.  A History of Congregational Independency in Scotland,  James MacLehose & Sons, Glasgow, 1900.

Savage, Anne.  The Anglo-Saxon Chronicles, Salamander Books, London, 2002.

Schaff, Philip.  History of the Christian Church, T.&T. Clark, Edinburgh, 1900.

Shepherd, J.W.  The Church, the Falling Away and the Reformation.

Smellie, Alexander.  Men of the Covenant, Banner of Truth Trust, Edinburgh, 1960.

Stevenson, Dwight E.  Walter Scott Voice of the Golden Oracle, Christian Board of Publications, St Louis, Missouri, 1946.

Thomson, David M.  Let Sects and Parties Fall, Berean Press, London, 1980.

Wade, John (Ed.).  Pioneers of the Restoration Movement, Standard Publishing, Cincinnati, Ohio, 1966.

Walker, Williston.  A History of the Christian Church, T.&T. Clark, Edinburgh, 1947.

Watters, A.C.  History of the British Churches of Christ, Berean Press, Birmingham, England, 1948.

West, Earle Irvin.  Search for the Ancient Order, Gospel Advocate, Nashville, 1949.

Womack, Morris M.  The Church Through the Ages, R.B. Sweet Co. Inc. Austin, Texas, 1965.

Yuille, George.  History of Baptists in Scotland, Baptist Union of Scotland, Glasgow, 1926.

### Booklets, Pamphlets, Tracts, Etc.

An Account of the Life and Character of Mr. John Glas, Edinburgh, 1813.

Alexander, William Lindsay.  Memoirs of the Life and Writings of Ralph Wardlaw D.D., Edinburgh, 1856.

An account of the Proceedings of the Society for Propagating the Gospel at Home, 1799

Athearn, C.R.  The Religious Education of Alexander Campbell.

Bennett, J.  Memoirs of the Life of the Rev. David Bogue, London, 1827.

Blair, James.  Errors of the Campbellites, 1840.

Borden, E.M. & Showalter, G.H.P.  Church History Showing the Origin of the Church of Christ.

Campbell, Alexander.  Memoir of Elder Thomas Campbell.

The Case of James Smith, late minister at Newburn and of Robert Ferrier, late minister at Largo, Truly Represented and Defended, Glasgow, 1816.

Coupar, W.J.  Scottish Revivals, Dundee, 1918.

Davis, M.M.  How the Disciples Began and Grew.

Davis, M.M.  The Restoration of the Nineteenth Century.

Erskine, John.  Signs of the Times Considered, Edinburgh, 1742.

Escott, Harry.  Beacons of Independency: Religion and Life in Strathbogie and Upper Garioch in the 19th Century, Huntly, 1940.

Ewing, Greville.  A Memoir of Barbara Ewing, Glasgow, 1829.

Ewing, Greville.  Facts and Documents Respecting the Connections which have subsisted between Robert Haldane Esq. and Greville Ewing, Glasgow, 1809.

Gilmour, David.  Reminiscences of the Pend Folk, Paisley, 1873.

Glas, John.  Works in V Volumes, Perth, 1782.

Grant, Peter.  Treatise on Baptism, Aberdeen, 1827.

Fleming, D.H.  The Scottish Reformation, London, 1910.

Haldane, Elizabeth S.  The Scotland of Our Fathers, A Study of Scottish Life in the 19th Century, London, 1933.

Haldane, James A. The Celebration of the Lord's Supper Every Lord's Day by the Late Mr. Randall, Mr Glas to Continuation of Mr. Glas' Narrative, Edinburgh, 1729.

Haldane, James A. Letters to a friend containing Strictures on a Recent Publication upon Primitive Christianity, Edinburgh, 1820.

Haldane, James A. Journal of a Tour through the Northern Counties of Scotland and the Orkney Isles in Autumn 1797, Edinburgh, 1798.

Haldane, James A. Observations on Forbearance, Edinburgh, 1811.

Haldane, James, A. Observations on the Association of Believers; Mutual Exhortation; the Apostolic Mode of Teaching ; Qualification and Support of Elders; Spiritual gifts etc, Edinburgh, 1808.

Haldane, James A. Reasons for a Change of Sentiment on the Subject of Baptism, Edinburgh, 1808.

Haldane, James A. Remarks on Mr. Jones Review of Observations on Forbearance, Edinburgh, 1812.

Haldane, James A. (Ed.) The Scripture Magazine, Edinburgh, 1809-13.

Haldane James A. Two Letters to Dr. Chalmers on His Proposal for Increasing the Number of Churches in Glasgow, Glasgow, 1818.

Haldane, Robert. Address to the Public concerning Political Opinions and Plans lately Adopted to Promote religion in Scotland, Edinburgh, 1800.

Hannah, W.H.  Thomas Campbell, Seceder and Christian Union Advocate.

Henderson, H.F.  The Religious Controversies of Scotland, Edinburgh, 1905.

Hill, Rowland.  Journal through the North of England and Parts of Scotland, London, 1799.

Hislop, David.  Congregationalism in the Border District, 1798-1898.

Hornsby, J.T.  John Glas, unpublished thesis, Edinburgh University School of Divinity.

Inglis, Henry D. Discourse on Ethiopian Eunuch, Edinburgh, 1790.

Innes, William.  Comprehensive View of the Origin and Tenets of the Baptists, 1821.

Innes, William.  Eugenio and Epenetus or Conversations Regarding Infant Baptism, Edinburgh, 1811.

Innes, William.  Reasons for Separating from the Church of Scotland, Dundee, 1804.

Jamieson, John.  Remarks on the Rev. Rowland Hill's Journal, Edinburgh, 1799.

Johnstone, Francis.  Baptism is Dipping, (104pp) London, 1865.

Johnstone, Francis.  Infant Baptism Not Christian Baptism (108pp) London, 1851.

Kershner, Frederick D. Restoration Handbook.

Kettle, Robert G. Baptism, (Two pamphlets) Glasgow, 1838.

Kinniburgh, Robert. Fathers of Independency in Scotland, Edinburgh, 1851.

Lindsay, James B. Baptism, Dundee.

Lockwood, David G. (Ed.) Christian Quarterly Magazine, 1832-37.

Lockwood, David G. The Testament of Baptism, (8pp) Glasgow, 1820.

Matheson, J.J. A Memoir of Greville Ewing, London, 1847.

MacInnes, J. The Evangelical Movement in the Highlands of Scotland 1688-1800, Aberdeen, 1951.

Maclean, Archibald. Christ's Commission Illustrated (328pp), Glasgow, 1786.

Maclean, Archibald. Church, Pastoral office and the Lord's Supper, 1801.

Maclean, Archibald. Conversations Between a Baptist and a Seceder, 1798.

Maclean, Archibald. Defence of Believer's Baptism, Edinburgh, 1777.

Maclean, Archibald. Nature and Import of Baptism (84pp), Edinburgh, 1786.

McCallister, Lester G. Thomas Campbell: A Man of the Book.

McGavin, James.  A Concise Abstract of the Faith, Hope and Practice of the Old Scots Independents, 1814.

McGavin, James.  Historical Sketches of the Old Scots Independents and the Inghamite Churches with the Correspondence that led to their Union, Colne, 1814.

McKerrow, John.  History of the Secession Church, Edinburgh, 1843.

McLean, Archibald.  Thomas and Alexander Campbell.

McNair, Robert.  Christian Baptism Spiritual Not Ritual, Edinburgh, 1855.

McPherson, James C.  Baptism: a Scriptural Enquiry, Peterhead, 1899.

Morrison, G.H.  Memoirs of Thomas Boston, Edinburgh, 1899.

Mursell, Walter.  Christian Baptism, Glasgow, 1909.

Philip, The Life, Times and Missionary Enterprises of the Rev. John Campbell, London, 1841.

Pirie, Alexander.  Dissertation on Baptising, Edinburgh, 1806.

Records of the Scottish Church History Society.

Reports of the Society for the Propagation of the Gospel at Home which are subjoined a Letter from Mr Haldane, Edinburgh, 1802.

Rowe, John F.  History of Reformatory Movements.

Shirreff, William. Lectures on Baptism (232pp), Edinburgh, 1845.

Sinclair, Sir William. Collection of Hymns and Spiritual Songs with Memoir, Edinburgh, 1847.

Struthers, G. A History of the Rise, Progress and Principles of the Relief Church, Glasgow, 1843.

Thompson, G.L.S. The Origins of Congregationalism in Scotland, Unpublished Thesis, Edinburgh University.

Thompson, Richard W. Benjamin Ingham and the Inghamites, Kendal, 1958.

Walker, N.L. Religious Life in Scotland from the Reformation to the Present Day, London, 1888.

Watt, James. Infant Baptism Unchristian, Dublin 1797.

Watt, James. Plain Proof that Public Creeds Involve Doctrines Erroneous and Intolerant, Glasgow, 1796.

William, Ken. The Hard and Dry Argument: in Answer to the Writer of "Baptism not Immersion," Irvine, 1822.

Wilson, Patrick. Origin and Progress of the Scots Baptist Churches from their Rise in 1765 to 1834 (100pp), Edinburgh, 1844.

*Author's note: the above are drawn from references in the bibliography section of many books on church history which are now out of print. Some of these are in the collections of the National Library of Scotland, George IV Bridge, Edinburgh and Edinburgh University School of Divinity, the Mound, Edinburgh. They are included by way of reference for future researchers. Notice the volume of writing on the issues of evangelism, baptism and church organisation from 1770 to 1850.*